Wakefield Press

DANTE'S INFERNO

About the Author

Enrico Mercuri is an Adjunct Professor in the School of Computer Science and Engineering, UNSW Sydney where he leads research, and co-supervises doctoral students. As a lawyer he has contributed to the drafting and interpretation of Australian Federal taxation law.

Enrico's formation included having Dante's *Inferno* read to him by his mother in his early years. This was followed by formal education in which he was awarded the university medal in Italian and wrote an Honours dissertation on Dante. He committed to only ever read the Divine Comedy in the original vernacular or in Italian. In 2022, for completeness and comparative assessment, Enrico elected to include English translations in his research.

In keeping with his contemporary approach to academic research, Enrico maintains a parallel programme at UNSW Sydney that employs data analytics. It is being utilised to identify and comparatively analyse the poetic form between the original and various English translations of the Divine Comedy. This analysis will culminate in subsequent publications.

About the Illustrator

David Blaiklock is Program Director of the Illustration and Animation program which he founded in 2018 at the University of South Australia (UniSA). As a university educator David has received a Distinguished Teaching Award from the Australian Council of University Art and Design Schools (ACAUDS) and a Citation for Outstanding Contribution to Student Learning from the Australian Office for Learning and Teaching.

David's design practice is internationally recognised, including Beijing Opera Art International Poster Biennale (2024), Shenzhen International Poster Festival, China (2023), International Eco-poster Triennial "the 4th Block", Ukraine, Hong Kong International Poster Triennial (2010), awarded Gold and Bronze, Adelaide Fringe 2009 National Poster Competition and 2006 Australian Poster Annual.

In terms of academic research, David focusses on cross cultural communication, social advocacy, and the nature of expertise within Illustration professional practice and education. In line with these interests, the illustrations developed for this translation of Dante's Inferno have contributed to doctoral research into Illustration professional practice which examines the nature of 'vision', 'visual language' and 'empathy' as forms of Illustration expertise.

Dante's Inferno

Enrico Mercuri

Illustrated by David Blaiklock

Wakefield Press

Wakefield Press
16 Rose Street
Mile End
South Australia 5031
www.wakefieldpress.com.au

First published 2024

Copyright © Enrico Mercuri, 2024

Illustrations Copyright © David Blaiklock, 2024

All rights reserved. This book is copyright. Apart from any fair dealing for the purposes of private study, research, criticism or review, as permitted under the Copyright Act, no part may be reproduced without written permission. Enquiries should be addressed to the publisher.

Text designed and typeset by Jesse Pollard, Wakefield Press

ISBN 978 1 92304 261 2

 A catalogue record for this book is available from the National Library of Australia

 Wakefield Press thanks Coriole Vineyards for continued support

Dedication

To my daughter Isabella Georgina for the marvel.
Given your interest in judicial pronouncements,
I remind you that Dante wrote the following:

> Le leggi son, ma chi pon mano ad esse?
> Nullo, però che 'l pastor che procede,
> rugumar può, ma non ha l'unghie fesse;
>
> per che la gente, che sua guida vede
> pur a quel ben fedire ond' ella è ghiotta,
> di quel si pasce, e più oltre non chiede.

Purgatorio Canto XVI, 97–102.

In memoriam

Frances Cufar.
A kind soul. A generous spirit. A keen intellect.

Contents

Introduction	*viii*
Canto I	1
Canto II	9
Canto III	17
Canto IV	25
Canto V	33
Canto VI	41
Canto VII	49
Canto VIII	57
Canto IX	65
Canto X	73
Canto XI	81
Canto XII	89
Canto XIII	97
Canto XIV	105
Canto XV	113
Canto XVI	121
Canto XVII	129
Canto XVIII	137
Canto XIX	145
Canto XX	153

Canto XXI	161
Canto XXII	171
Canto XXIII	179
Canto XXIV	187
Canto XXV	195
Canto XXVI	203
Canto XXVII	211
Canto XXVIII	219
Canto XXIX	227
Canto XXX	235
Canto XXXI	243
Canto XXXII	251
Canto XXXIII	259
Canto XXXIV	267

Introduction

This *Cantica* is a study of horror that has thrived for over 700 years. I propose it to any reader, religious or not, as a presentation of the nature of evil, its cause and effect, limitless variation and ease of attainment. Dante's poetic work condenses and presents a universal perspective relevant to expressions of hell as we see them today. I hope you find it readable and meaningful.

My intention for this translation is to make Dante's masterpiece accessible to a contemporary readership. Dante chose to write the Divine Comedy in the vernacular of the common people rather than the Latin of the educated class. The English I here use aims to mirror that intent in its goal of achieving expression that is at once contemporary, idiomatic, and fluid. It represents the output of a lifetime's interest and research.

Stylistically and structurally and therefore rhythmically, I have sought to capture the flow of the original text. This has included appreciating dialectal coincidence and its cadence outside the Tuscan vernacular while examining the wording of the original text.

Methodologically, it has meant placing English in the broader dialectal context. By creating this associative environment, English word choice is also given the best opportunity for accuracy and depth of expression. This has led to inclusion of words characteristic of the Australian vernacular.

Furthermore, in supporting research for this translation, I have given due consideration to the commentaries of various authors since the fourteenth century including and not limited to: Giovanni Boccaccio (1313–1375), Francesco da Buti (1324–1405), Benvenuto

Introduction

da Imola (1330–1388), Cristoforo Landino (1424–1498), and Anna Maria Chiavacci Leonardi (1927–2014).

Moreover, since 2022 I have comparatively considered the English texts beginning with Longfellow, Musa and Carey, and extending to Hollander. Relevantly and by contrast, I avoid what to the modern reader can be the laboriousness of the earlier English translations, and some of the now somewhat anachronistic idioms of the twentieth century.

In the spirit of Dante's time, I also acknowledge the contextual contribution made by Italian dialects while growing up in Australia: Neapolitan, Calabrian, Venetian, Sicilian and others including Romanesque sub variations (*Bassianese*, *Terracinese* and *Sezzese*).

Up to the turn of the twenty first century, the dialects heard in Australia remained suspended in time and retained a level of authenticity and usage now rarely found. Although their presence in contemporary Australian culture has significantly diminished, the echo remains and has provided me a fertile and diverse etymological backdrop to the work.

To these speakers from the past I extend heartfelt thanks, in particular: Salvatore and Nina Palombi (*eh comane, Erico è zego ma è capocciuto!*); Natale and Felice Orlando; Angelo Vial and Mario Beltrame.

Finally, I express my appreciation to Dr. Giuseppe Bolognese whose extempore recitations of *La Divina Commedia* for entire university lectures have never been matched. Without my exposure to such erudition, this text would not have arrived at the form it has.

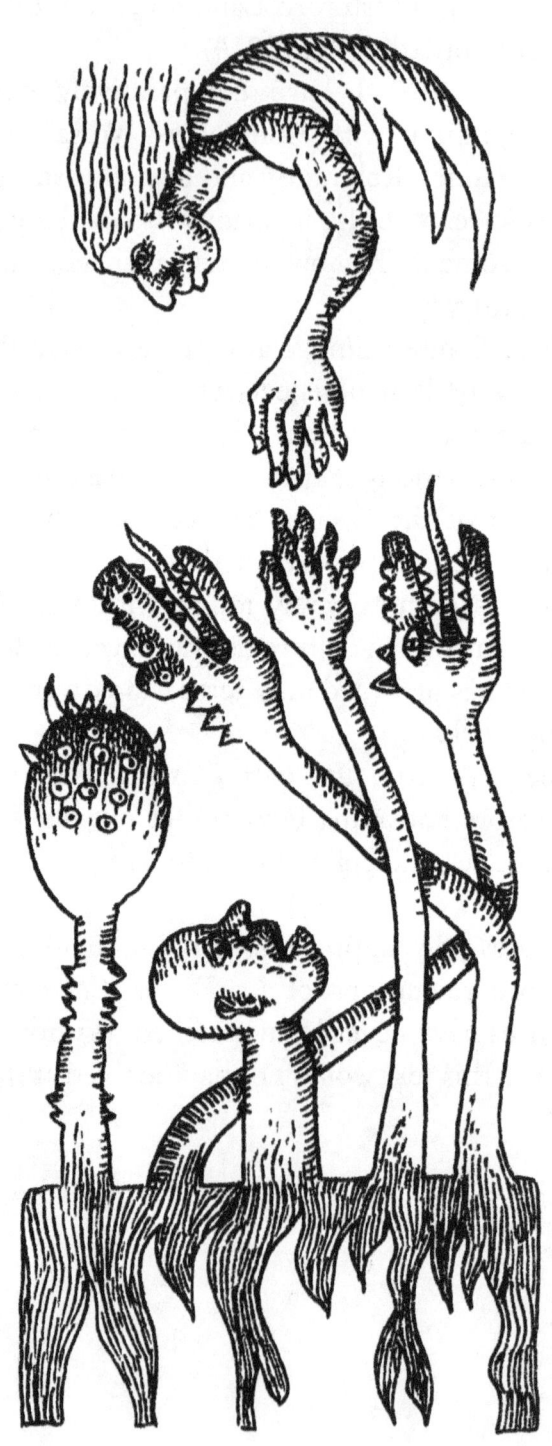

Canto I

This Canto sets the scene for Dante the pilgrim's horrific and sublime journey into the extremes of the human condition. Dante experiences a death-like crisis in middle age that compels him to confront the internal horrors that prevent him going directly to the sublime light he can see above. These take the form of the three beasts he encounters as he emerges from the dark valley of his soul. They are such a threat that death is imminent should he pursue the course, so he retreats towards the valley. Unexpectedly, a figure appears to whom Dante appeals and who responds. He is Virgil, *dramatis personae*, Roman poet, metaphor for the faculty of reason and companion for the part of the epic journey in which reason has a place: hell and purgatory. Virgil offers travelling away from there into the eternal places: one where souls hopelessly screech desiring a second death; another where suffering continues, assuaged by hope; and the third from which Virgil has been expressly excluded for which, Dante consenting, a greater guide will become responsible. Dante agrees and the great pilgrimage begins.

Dante's Inferno

Midway through our life journey
I found myself in a dark forest,
having lost life's true path.

Oh how painful it is to tell how it was,
a forest wild, intractable and impassable
that it renews the memory of that fear!

It is so bitter that death is barely worse;
but so to address the good I there found,
I will speak of other things I observed.

I cannot precisely recount how I entered it,
so immersed was I in that sleep
while abandoning the way of truth.

But once at the foot of the mount,
where the valley that afflicted
my heart with fear had ended,

looking up high I saw its summit already
clothed by that celestial body's light
which directs each along every pathway.

It was then that the fear began to settle,
having stayed in the depths of my heart
for the night I had spent in such anguish.

And like he who, breathless, leaves
the sea and on reaching the shore,
turns fixing on the dangerous water,

so too my soul, still in flight, turned
back to gaze again at the path
that has never left a mortal alive.

Canto I

Having rested my weary body some,
I went again along the deserted slope,
my lower foot being the firmer one.

When oh, near onset of the incline,
a lithe lightning-fast leopard,
that was covered in spotted fur;

would not spare me its presence,
indeed so impeded my progress,
more than once I turned to return.

The time was very early morning,
the sun was rising with those stars
present with it when divine love

first moved the beauteous things;
as time of day and spring season
did give me reason to have hope

in that beast with the mottled skin,
but not so far that fear did not come
from the vision of a lion that appeared.

He seemed to be moving against me
with head high and rabid with hunger,
that it seemed even the air shuddered.

and a she wolf that in her leanness
appeared imbued with all cravings,
having already led many to misery,

burdened me with such anguish
from the fear of its presence,
that I lost all hope for the summit.

And similar to one who readily gains,
and arriving at the time of losing,
in all thoughts cries and is saddened;

so rendered me the beast without peace,
that, approaching me a step at a time,
nudged me below to where sunlight is silent.

While I careered toward the low place,
before my eyes appeared one whose
voice in the long silence seemed distant.

When I saw him in the place of abandon,
I called to him "Have mercy on me,
whether you be shadow, or mortal man!".

He answered, "not man, though I was,
and my parents were Lombards,
each of them a native of Mantua.

Born under Caesar, though in latter years,
I lived in Rome under the good Augustus
at the time of false and lying gods.

I was a poet, who sang of the just deeds
of the son of Anchises, who came from Troy,
after the proud Ilium was burned down.

But why do you return to such anguish?
why do you not climb the joyous mount
that is the source and reason for all bliss?".

"So, are you the Virgil that is the source
from whom flows such river of eloquence?",
replied I with self conscious countenance.

Canto I

"Oh honour of and light for other poets,
may I profit from long study and great
love that drove me to search your works.

You are my Master and my author,
It is from you only that I gained
the elegant style that gave me honour.

See that beast causing me to turn back;
save me from her, oh great sage, for she
makes my veins and pulse tremble to the core".

"You will need to take another way",
he answered after seeing my tears,
"to save yourself from this savage place;

for this beast, of whom you complain,
allows no-one to travel along her path
and she so resists till she kills them;

and has a nature so maleficent and vicious,
that she can never satisfy her greed, and
after her meal is more famished than before.

Many are the animals with which she copulates
and many more to come, until the Greyhound
will come who will make her die violently.

He will not feed on landholding or alloy,
but wisdom, love and virtue,
and be birthed between *feltro* and *feltro*.

He will save humbled Italy for whom
did perish the virgin Cammilla, Euryalus and
Turnus, and Nisus from their wounds.

He will hunt her from city to city
until he drives her back into hell,
where jealousy first unleashed her.

So I regard it in your best interest
to follow me, I will be your guide, taking
you from here through the eternal place;

where you will hear the desperate cries,
you will see the ancient damned spirits,
each screeching wanting a second death;

and you will see those who are content
in the fire, because hope remains to join
the beatified ones at the appointed time.

To whom if you wish to then go further,
a soul more meritorious for it than I
will I leave you with upon my departure;

indeed that Emperor who reigns above,
because I was rebellious to his law,
decreed to deny me entry to His city.

He is sovereign everywhere governing there;
For there is his city and sublime throne:
oh happy are those whom he selects!".

And I: "Poet, I pray in the name
of that God which you knew not,
so I may flee this evil and worse,

that you guide me to where you now say,
so that I may see the gate of St. Peter
and those you describe in such misery".

Then he moved, and I pursued closely.

Canto II

Having commenced their journey, Virgil converses with Dante who is gripped by self-doubt as to his merit in receiving such privilege reserved for great historical figures. Dante appeals to Virgil's wisdom that exceeds his ability to express himself. Virgil, objectively and without condemnation, diagnoses Dante's hesitancy as cowardice. To relieve Dante of the fear, Virgil recounts how his intervention came about in the heavenly realm. While he was in hell's first circle of Limbo, Beatrice came and appealed to the poet to assist Dante for whom all may already have been lost following the confrontation with the beasts. Virgil promptly agrees but wants to better understand the motivation behind Beatrice's request. She explains that the Mother of God had taken pity on Dante and asked Saint Lucia to intervene. Saint Lucia had then approached Beatrice due to Dante's great love for her. Beatrice in turn descended to Limbo to give effect to the request. Hearing this, Dante is once again motivated to continue on the savage path.

Dante's Inferno

It was dusk and the darkening air
was freeing earth's creatures
from their toil; and I on my own

prepared to sustain the travail
of the journey and of the sorrow,
that the unerring memory will recount.

Oh muses and high genius help me now;
oh memory stamped with what I saw,
here your noble nature will be unveiled.

So I began: "My Poet and my guide,
weigh up if my virtue is capable, before
entrusting me with this arduous journey.

It is true as you say that Silvius' father
while still corruptible, to immortality
travelled and did so whilst still sensate.

Therefore, if the adversary of all evil
privileged him, thinking of the great progeny
yet to issue, the who and what he was,

it is not improper to a man of intellect;
as predestined by supreme Heaven to be
the father of Rome and of its empire:

each of which, to tell the truth
was established as the holy site
where sits great Peter's successor.

Due to this voyage you memorialise,
he heard things that brought about
his victory and so the papal mantle.

Canto II

The chosen instrument then went
to give affirmation to that Faith –
entry to the pathway to salvation.

But why should I go? Who permits it?
I am not Eneas, nor am I Paul; neither
I nor others regard me as entitled.

Therefore, if I concede to come, I fear
the coming may be reckless. You sage,
comprehend more than I do rationalise".

As he who no longer wants what he once
wanted and ideates intent in new thought,
so that he abandons what first initiated,

so too I became on that dark slope,
as I mentally abandoned the voyage
that was so compelling at the onset.

"If I understand your words correctly",
replied the noble shadow of the great one,
"Your soul is victim of the cowardice;

which many times so impedes a man
distracting from honourable enterprise,
as animal withdraws from a false image.

So that you may be free of any such fear,
I will tell you why I came and what I heard
in the first moment that I felt your pain.

I was with those in a state of suspension,
a woman so blessed and beautiful called,
that I exhorted she command her wishes.

Her eyes shone more than any star and
she began in manner elegant and sweet,
communicating words in angelic voice:

'Oh courteous Mantuan soul whose
fame is still known in the world,
and will continue for its duration,

he that is my friend but not fortune's
is so impeded on the deserted incline
that because of fear is turning back;

and I fear that he may be already lost,
given what I heard of him in heaven,
that my move to rescue comes too late.

Now run, and with your eloquence
and all else necessary to his survival,
go to his aid so I may be consoled.

I who am sending you am Beatrice;
here from that place I desire to return to;
love having moved me now to speak.

When I find myself before my Lord
I will often sing your praises to Him'.
She stopped there, and then I began:

'Oh woman of virtue through whom
the human species overcomes all that
held within the lunar sky's gyrations,

your command is so welcome that
if I'd already obeyed, it would be tardy;
say no more than what you wish done.

Canto II

But tell me why it is that you do not fear
descending down here to this centre
from that furthest heaven you yearn for'.

'Since you wish to know so deeply,
I will explain briefly', she replied,
'why I do not fear entering here.

One must fear only those things
that have the power to cause harm;
not others, as they are not fearsome.

God by His Grace made me impervious,
so that your misery does not touch me,
nor can any flame of this fire assault me.

A noble woman in Heaven lamenting
at this impediment to which I send you,
has suspended severe high judgment.

She invoked Lucia to advocate her plea
and said: your faithful is now in need
of you, and it is to you I commend him.

Lucia, being the enemy of all cruelty
rose quickly, moving to where I was,
seated next to the ancient Rachel.

She said: Beatrice, very praise of God
why not succour he who loved you so
as to rise above the vulgar masses?

Do you not hear the anguish in his crying,
do you not see death attacking him more
in waters even storms at sea cannot vie with?

Dante's Inferno

No-one on earth was more responsive
to pursue their gain or flee their harm
as I having those words spoken to me,

and I descended here from the celestial
seat trusting in your noble words that
honour you and whoever has heard them'.

Having reasoned with these words,
she took her leave with glistening eyes,
which induced me to come more quickly.

So I came to you exactly as she wished:
and freed you from that beast who denied
you the quicker way to the blessed hill.

So: what is it? Why? Why hesitate?
Why nurture such cowardness of heart,
Why not display courage and strength,

given that those three blessed women
care for your welfare in Heaven's court
and my words promise so much good?".

As little flowers in the night's frost
bent and closed, brighten in the sun,
and rise in full flower on their stems,

so was I restored from a weary soul,
and such good daring filled my heart
that I began speaking, emboldened:

"oh how pitying is she who aided me!
and you courteous one quickly obeying
the infallible words she did put to you!

Canto II

Your words have disposed my heart
with such desire to come with you,
that I return to my original intention.

So proceed, as our wills have one wish:
you are my guide, Lord and teacher".
So I spoke; and when he began to walk,

I entered the arduous and savage path.

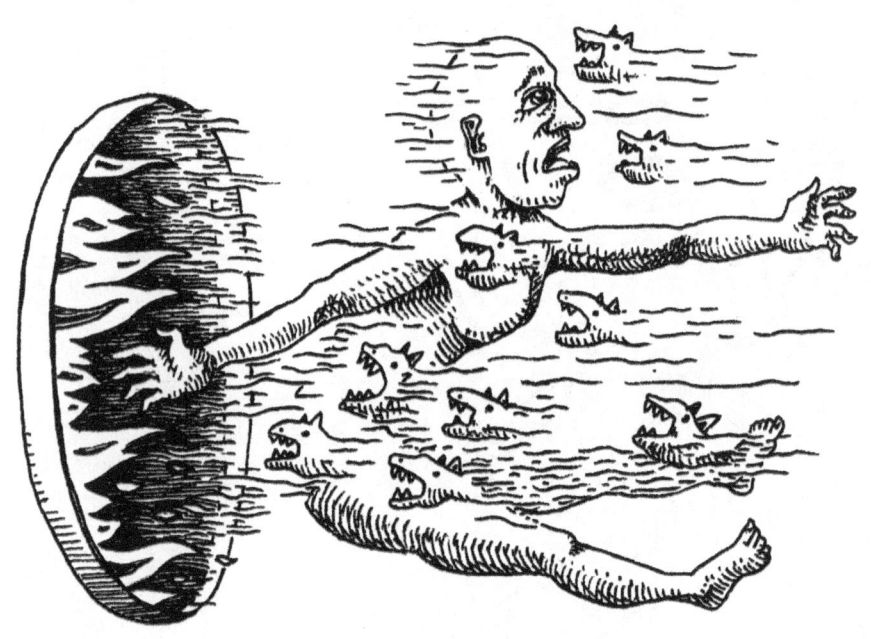

Canto III

The third Canto opens with the stark reality of the entrance to hell. The sign above the doorway leaves nothing to the imagination as to its origins, purpose and permanence. Dante soon experiences the shrieks and erratic mixture of sounds all borne out of unremitting violence. These are souls who are not only in excruciating pain but bear the ignominy of having been rejected by both Heaven and hell. This is due to their inability to commit themselves to anything substantive in life. They neither excelled nor failed but stood for themselves – Heaven rejects them as they would diminish its beauty; and hell snubs any association as it may detract from the utter despair of its own. Virgil echoes this, adding there is not even a memory of their existence and leaves them in anonymity and irrelevance by truncating further discussion. Dante recognises some but does not name them. The travellers then arrive at the river Acheron, where all souls congregate in obedience and terror to face transportation across it by the ferryman of Greek mythology, Charon. There they will face judgment and allocation within hell itself. Suddenly, a violent wind dashes Dante into unconsciousness.

"THROUGH ME ENTER THE AFFLICTED CITY,
THROUGH ME ENTER ETERNAL PAIN,
THROUGH ME ENTER AMONG THE DAMNED.

MY SUBLIME CREATOR MOVED BY JUSTICE;
CREATED ME BY DIVINE POWER,
SUPREME WISDOM AND PRIMAL LOVE.

BEFORE ME THERE WAS NOTHING THAT
WAS NOT ETERNAL, AND I AM ETERNAL.
ABANDON ALL HOPE, YE WHO ENTER".

These dark and dismal written words
I observed upon the doorway pediment;
and I said: "Master their meaning is hard".

And he answered me in expert fashion:
"Here we must relinquish all wariness;
any cowardice must die here and now.

We have arrived at the place I told you of
where you will see the dolorous damned
who have lost their goodness of intellect".

Then, after placing his hand on mine
with a smiling face comforting me,
he led me into the things kept secret.

Herein sighing, crying and howling
echoed in the air of a starless sky,
so that at the onset I began to cry.

Strange languages, awful utterances, words
of pain, angry imprecation, voices thunderous
and muffled, with sounds of hands slapping

Canto III

causing a tumult spiralling about
constantly in that eternal darkness,
as sand swirled by a twisting tornado.

And I whose mind was full of doubt,
said: "Master, what is that I hear?
who are they so conquered by pain?".

And he replied: "This is the miserable state
had by the sad spirits of they who lived
without infamy and without distinction.

They meld with that contemptible choir
of angels who were neither rebellious nor
faithful to God, but stood for themselves.

Heaven cast them out to avoid loss of beauty,
nor does the depth of Inferno welcome them,
as the lost may gain glory from their presence".

And I: "Master, what is so grievous
to them that they lament so loudly?".
He answered: "I will explain briefly.

These cannot hope in true death,
and their blind life is so ignoble,
that any other soul's destiny do crave.

The world disallows any memory of them;
mercy and justice hold them in disdain:
let's not discuss them, but glance and walk on".

And I, while looking on, saw an ensign
that was whirling and moving so rapidly
that it seemed incapable of any resting;

and behind it followed a limitless host
of which I would never have believed
that death had so many left undone.

Having recognised some of them, I saw
and knew the shadow of he who by his
cowardice committed the great refusal.

I instantly understood and was sure
that this was the sect of the vile ones,
disdained by God and by His enemies.

These disgraced, who never truly lived,
were naked and relentlessly stung
by the circling flies and wasps there.

They bloodily lined their faces leaving
drops, mingled with tears, at their feet
to be consumed by repugnant worms.

And then redirecting my gaze farther on,
I saw spirits gathered at a great river bank;
at which I said: "Master, now grant that

I may know who these are, and what law
drives their evident desire to cross,
that I am observing in this twilight".

And he replied: "this will be clear
when we have come to a halt there
at the miserable shore of Acheron".

Then embarrassed with downcast eyes,
fearing my words may be unwelcome,
I remained silent till reaching the river.

Canto III

And behold approaching on a boat was
a decrepit old man with white beard,
screaming: "Woe to you, depraved souls!

Abandon all hope to ever see Heaven:
I come to take you to the other bank
to eternal darkness of flame and ice.

And you there, oh mortal one
move off from these who are dead".
But then seeing I was not leaving,

he said: "By other way, by other ports
will you travel and land, not here:
as a lighter vessel must carry you".

And my Master: "Charon, stop grinding:
this is willed above where all is done
as decided, so just hold your tongue".

So were quietened the bearded cheeks
of the helmsman of the livid swamp,
with eyes encircled by wheels aflame.

But those spirits naked and worn,
lost colour and teeth chattered, upon
hearing their fate in such cruel words.

So were cursing God and parents,
humanity, place and time, seed
of their seeding and origin of birth.

Then they all assembled tightly packed,
crying in despair on the infernal bank
that awaits all men that do not fear God.

Dante's Inferno

The demon Charon, eyes of burning coal
motioning to them, collecting them all;
beating any procrastinator with the oar.

As when the Autumn leaves fall
one after another, until the branch
sees its coverings return to earth,

Similarly did the worst seed of Adam
one by one toss themselves from the bank,
responding as birds to hunter's lure.

Then they travel along the dark waters,
and before disembarking on the other side,
another crowd forms again on this side.

"My son", said the courteous Master,
"all who die attracting God's anger
from all the earth convene here;

and readily board to cross the river,
as are compelled by divine justice,
such that fear into desire transforms.

Through here no good soul passes;
so if Charon complains of you, grasp
well what these words mean for you".

Immediately hence, the dark surroundings
quaked so much that even now the fear
in my mind leaves me in a cold sweat.

The landscape of tears unleashed a wind,
from which blazed a blood red light
that deeply overwhelmed my senses;

and I fell as a man overcome by sleep.

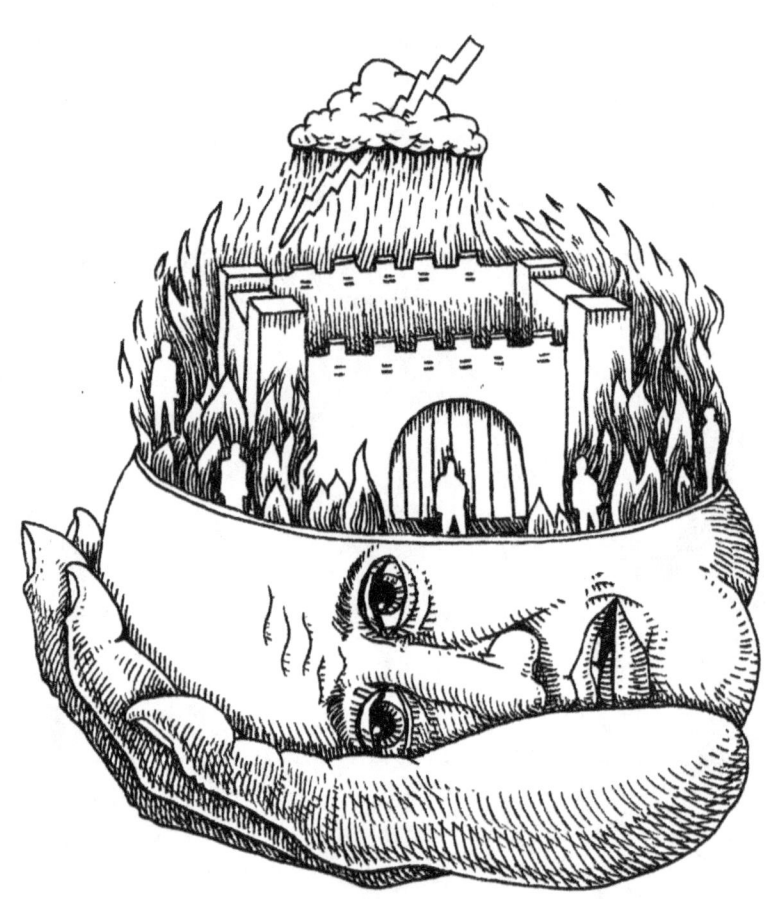

Canto IV

Dante is woken by heavy thunder to profound, continuous lamentation issuing from the abyss. He and Virgil descend into it. This is the first circle of hell in which are found those who died without possessing Faith and who eternally desire it in the knowledge it can now never be achieved. These souls are not subject to the violence and agony found in later circles, only this deprivation. Dante discovers that Virgil is one of these and witnesses the marvellous scene of the reunion of his guide with other exceptional personages from history: Homer, Horace, Ovid and Lucan. These four poets unite with Virgil in discourse and after some time all turn towards Dante, motioning for him to join them. Here we witness Dante the poet declaring his status through Dante the character. Once the select group enters the castle, a number of other famous people are noted that include: Electra, Aeneas, Caesar, Saladin, Aristotle, Plato, Orpheus, Cicero, Avicenna, and Averroes. The poise of this Canto is in marked contrast to the anguish of the remaining Canti of *Inferno*.

Dante's Inferno

The deep sleep in my head was interrupted
by a heavy thunderclap, such that I regained
my senses brusquely as a person startled;

and with rested eyes surveying, I stood
up straight focussing and observing
to best understand where I now was.

Indeed, I found myself at the edge
of the valley of abysmal sorrow that
reaps cataclysmic infinite howling.

It was so dark, deep and cloudy
that, though straining my gaze,
I could not discern anything down there.

"Now we descend to the blind world",
began the poet with pallid face.
"I will go first, and you will follow".

And I, now aware of his paleness
said: "How can I come, if you fear going
who are my comfort against doubting?".

And he to me: "the anguish of souls
down here doth colour my face,
with empathy you perceive as fear.

Come, as the long road presses".
So he proceeded and thus led me
into the first ring encircling the abyss.

Here, as best could be grasped by listening,
there were no tears, merely sighing
resonating through the eternal air;

Canto IV

this came from grief without torment,
had by hordes, large and many consisting
of infants and of women and of men.

The good Master said: "Do you not ask
which spirits are these that you see?
I want you to know, before advancing,

these did not sin; and if have merit,
it was lacking, as were not baptised,
the doorway to the faith you possess;

and if they preceded Christianity,
they did not adore God as due:
and of these I myself am one too.

For these defects and no other guilt,
are we lost, and are simply condemned
that without hope remain yet longing".

Great sorrow took my heart when I knew,
therefore, that people of such great merit
were suspended in that state of Limbo.

"Tell me, my Master, tell me Lord",
I began, to reassure myself about
that faith that defeats all error:

"has anyone left here, of their own merit
or that of another, to then attain holiness?"
And he, understanding my veiled words,

answered: "I was here but a short time,
when I saw enter one of mighty power,
crowned with the symbol of victory.

From us he took the soul of the first parent,
of his son Abel and also that of Noah,
and of Moses the obedient law giver;

of the Patriarch Abraham and King David,
Israel with his father and his children, with
Rachel, for whom he laboured so long,

and many others, and made them blest.
And I want you to know that before them,
no other human spirits were saved".

We did not stop our trek while he spoke,
but continued passing through the thicket,
by which I mean thicket of thronged spirits.

Not long had our walk progressed
beyond the summit, when I saw a fire
that lit up a hemisphere of darkness.

We were still quite well distant, but
not too far for me not to discern that
people of honour occupied that place.

"Oh you who exalt science and art,
who are these that are so honoured,
their condition setting them apart?".

And he to me: "the honoured status
that still resounds of them in your world,
gains favour in Heaven, distinguishing them".

In the meantime I heard a voice:
"All honour the illustrious poet:
his spirit since gone, now returns".

Canto IV

After the voice ceased and silence returned,
I saw four mighty spirits approach:
their visages neither sad nor happy.

The good Master began by saying:
"see he who holds a sword in hand,
preceding the others as if a monarch:

that is Homer the supreme poet;
followed by Horace the satirist;
third is Ovid and the last Lucan.

Since each and I hold in common
the one title sounded by that voice,
they bring me honour, and do well to do so".

So I saw gather the gracious school
of that Lord of most sublime song
soaring over the others as an eagle.

After talking somewhat among themselves,
they turned to me with accepting gestures
and my Master smiled at the sight of this;

and greater honour they bestowed on me,
as they embraced me as one of them,
so I was the sixth within such wisdom.

Then we proceeded towards the light,
speaking of things now best left unsaid,
such were the words fitting there and then.

We arrived at the foot of a spectacular castle,
surrounded by seven levels of high walls,
defended around it by a beautiful streamlet.

We crossed it as though on solid terrain;
I entered seven doors with these sages:
arriving at a meadow of fresh greenery.

There, souls composed and austere
in semblance of great authority did appear:
speaking sparingly with elegant voices.

We then gathered a little to one side,
on an incline, open and luminous,
from which we could see everyone.

There in front, on the glazed green,
the majestic spirits were shown to me,
whom I still feel exalted in having seen.

I saw Electra with many companions,
among whom I noted Hector and Aeneas,
Caesar armed, with sparrowhawk's eyes.

I saw Camilla and Penthesilea;
on the opposite side I saw King Latinus
who was seated with daughter Lavinia.

I saw that Brutus who ejected Tarquinius,
Lucretia, Julia, Marcia, and Cornelia;
and alone to one side I saw Saladin.

After having lifted my eyes a little higher,
I saw the Master of the knowledgeable
sitting among the philosophic family.

All admiring him, all honouring him:
there I saw Socrates and Plato,
who ahead of others were closest to him;

Canto IV

Democritus whose world view is chance,
Dïogenès, Anaxagoras, and Thales,
Empedoclès, Heraclitus and Zeno;

and I saw the talented classifier of plants,
I mean Dïascoride; then I saw Orpheus,
Tully and Linus and the moralist Seneca;

the geometer Euclid and Ptolemy,
Hippocrates, Avicenna and Galen,
Averroes, who wrote the great commentary.

I cannot recount the detail of all of them,
because my vast material spurs me on,
so often narration limits all of the facts.

The company of six depletes to two:
my sage Master takes me by other path,
away from still air, to where it shudders.

And I arrive in a part where nought is lucent.

Canto V

The horrors of hell become truly evident in this Canto. The pilgrim is confronted by the judge of the underworld in Greek mythology: Minos. This is hell's seat of judgment, where Minos listens to the willing confession of each lost soul and proceeds to condemn and sentence it to its proper place in hell. He confronts Dante, attempting to assert his authority at which Virgil retorts that Higher authority has already pre-determined that access to hell would be allowed them. Minos remains silent. Virgil and Dante continue. They enter a dark place savaged by violent gusts of wind that metaphorically represent the chaotic impulses of the sin of lust. Disorder reigns as the figures are eternally catapulted in every direction. Virgil points out more than one thousand of them to Dante, explaining their sinful history. Dante then notices and requests to speak to two of them: Paolo and Francesca. The two being brother and sister in law, were caught *in flagrante* by Francesca's husband who immediately dispensed with them, without their being able to repent. Their fate is to be eternally bonded and directionless at the mercy of whim, represented by the buffeting winds. Dante is overcome with sadness for them and collapses into unconsciousness.

In this way I descended from the first circle
to the second, which encloses less space
and such greater pain, driving the howling.

There stands Minos horribly, growling:
examining sins of they at the entrance;
judging and sentencing by twists of tail.

I mean that when the illegitimate soul
presents itself to him, it confesses all;
and he being the savant of sinfulness

decides in which location of hell it belongs;
he contorts his tail the number of times
enumerating the circle to precipitate into.

Before him are always crowds of souls:
going each in turn to their judgment,
confessing, hearing and being cast down.

"Oh you who come to the home of agony",
screamed Minos at me when he saw me,
halting the deliberation of his great office,

"beware of entering and whom you trust;
don't be fooled by width and ease of entry!".
My Master retorted: "why the screaming?

do not impede his already ordained entry:
it is willed above where what is wanted
is done, and you're to question no more".

Now the anguished voices begin
reaching my ear; now I have arrived
where great crying pummels me.

Canto V

I entered a place devoid of all light,
that bellows as the sea in a tempest,
when clashing winds do assault it.

The infernal storm, that never calms,
buffets the souls with its gusts;
tormenting by flipping and striking them.

When they arrive at the circle's precipice,
there begins shrieking, crying, lamenting;
cursing the power of the Divine almighty.

I understood that to this type of torment
are condemned the sinners of the flesh,
that submit conscience to lasciviousness.

And as starlings are borne by their wings
in winter, forming flocks tight and wide,
so does that wind hurl those evil spirits

here, there, down, up, it casts them;
they have no hope to comfort them,
neither of repose, nor even less suffering.

And as cranes break into their bugling,
whilst forming a long line in the sky,
so I saw coming near, while howling,

spirits being transported by that storm;
I then said: "Master, who are those
people castigated by the black tempest?".

"The first of those whom you wish
to know about", he then replied,
"was empress of many a language.

Dante's Inferno

She was so devoted to the vice of lust,
that she enshrined lust as licit at law,
to erase infamy into which she did fall.

She is Semiramìs of whom we read who
succeeded Ninus as his wife on the throne:
she governed the land the Sultan now rules.

The other is she who suicided for love,
and broke faith to the ashes of Sichaeus;
then there is the licentious Cleopatra.

You see Helen, over whom such long
hardship occurred, and see great Achilles,
who fought to the death for reason of love.

See Paris, Tristan"; more than a thousand
spirits he pointed out to me one by one,
who had departed this life for love.

Then, after having heard my teacher
name the ancient dames and knights,
pity took me and I became near insentient.

I began then by saying: "Poet, I would
gladly speak to those two going together,
who seem so weightless in the wind".

And he to me: "wait till they are closer
to us; and you then entice them by the
love driving them, and they will come".

Just as the wind bent them to us,
I spoke: "oh you burdened spirits,
come speak to us, unless denied!".

Canto V

As doves are called by a wish innate,
with firm raised wing to a sweet nest
through air driven by their will's behest;

so the two exited the crowd where Dido is,
coming towards us along the malignant air,
so strong and warm was my call to them.

"Oh gracious and benign mortal being
visiting through this blackened air we
who stained the earth in bloody hue,

if the king of the universe were a friend
we would pray to him you have peace,
given you show pity on our perverse ill.

Of whatever you wish to hear and speak,
we will listen and converse with you,
while the wind slows, as doing so now.

The land in which I was born sits
at the shore where the Po descends
as confluent streams to peacefulness.

Love which quickly enkindles a kind heart,
inflamed him here towards my beauty that
was stolen; in a manner which still ails me.

Love which doesn't permit it be unrequited,
took me with such pleasure of him, that
as you see, it still does not relinquish me.

Love carried us to the one death.
Caïna awaits who extinguished us".
These their words were borne thus.

Dante's Inferno

When I heard those offended spirits,
I lowered my gaze and held it so long
till the poet said: "what are you thinking?".

When I answered, I began: "Oh dear,
what sweet thoughts, what desire
brought these to their woeful passage".

Then I turned to them to speak,
and began: "Francesca, your sufferings
bring me tears of sadness and pity.

But tell me: at the time of sweet sighs,
what sign and in which way did love concede
for you to know of your hidden desires?".

And Francesca: "there is no greater sorrow
than to remember happy times when
in misery; as your master does well know.

But if knowing about the first root
of our love is what you much desire,
then I will reply as one tearfully telling.

One day, in reading for recreation
how Lancelot was gripped by love;
we were alone and unsuspecting.

More than once our eyes met during
that reading, and our faces lost colour;
but only at one point were we won over.

When we read of her smiling mouth
being kissed by so exalted a lover,
he, never to be divided from me,

Canto V

kissed my mouth trembling all over.
A Galeotto was that book and its author:
that day we did not read any further".

While one spirit was saying this,
the other cried; so that from pity
I swooned as if I was going to die.

And fell as a collapsing cadaver falls.

Canto VI

Dante regains consciousness to find himself in the third circle. Here the howling gluttonous are eternally lashed by relentless wind and rain and lie engulfed in filthy mud. They are guarded by the three-dog headed Cerberus that roars over and tears them apart. Virgil throws handfuls of the mud into its mouths that greedily gorge on and satiate it. So he and the Pilgrim make their way over the prostrated souls until one straightens itself upon recognising Dante. His name was Ciacco and he tells Dante of others whom Dante knows that are in even deeper hell. He also prophesises on the divisions of Florence and their outcome. A delightful moment of poetic sagacity is seen when Ciacco is unable to speak further and begins to relapse into his anguished impotence:[1]

He rolled his eyes and his gaze distorted;
looking at me a little he bowed his head:
crumpling alongside the other blind ones.

There is a dense pathos in his last glimpse of Dante which the reader perceives will be forever lost. It is a reminder by Dante of the ephemeral nature of life and permanence of the afterlife. The two continue their journey. Virgil then makes a statement about the relativistic nature of pleasure and pain following the Final Judgment. They arrive at a point to be faced with Pluto.

---

1. *Li occhi torse allora in biechi;*
   guardommi un poco e poi chinò la testa:
   cadde con essa a par de li altri ciechi.

Dante's Inferno

In regaining consciousness after its loss
at the pitiful state of the two in-laws,
which overwhelmed me with anguish,

new torments and new tormented
surrounded me, whichever way I moved
or turned, or upon which my gaze fixed.

I am in the third circle, that of rain
eternal, accursed, cold and violent;
never new in volume and substance.

Huge hail, murky water and snow
unleash torrentially in the gloom;
fouling the soil that bears them.

Cerberus, cruel and grotesque beast,
howls as a dog with his three throats
over those who wallow in that mire.

With bloody eyes, black unctuous beard
puffed belly and talons as hands;
scratches, flays and quarters the damned.

The rain makes them all howl like dogs;
in shielding one flank by exposing the other,
the disgraced impious turn this way and that.

When Cerberus, the great worm, saw us
he opened his mouths exposing his fangs;
and none of his members did not quake.

And my Master stretched out his hands,
taking mud and, holding handfuls of it,
threw them into the ravenous jaws.

Canto VI

In the same way as a barking dog craves,
and then after gulping its food quietens,
intent on and driven only to devour it,

so too did behave those lurid faces
of demon Cerberus, who thunders
at spirits such, they desire deafness.

We walked treading on souls beaten
by that heavy rain, placing our soles
on insubstantial but like human forms.

They were all lying down on the ground,
except one who sat up immediately
upon seeing us before him as we passed.

"Oh you being guided through this hell",
he said, "recognise me, if you are able:
as you were made before I was no more".

And I to him: "the anguish that you have
perhaps makes you unrecognisable to me,
so that it seems I have never known you.

So tell me who you are put in this such
awful place, and have punishment that
if any is greater, none is so repugnant".

And he to me: "your city that is so full
of envious striving taken beyond the brink,
hosted me during my mortal serenity.

You citizens nicknamed me Ciacco:
for my damning sin as a glutton,
as you see, I am wrecked by the rain.

And I, trist soul, am not alone, as all
these are subject to the same penalty
for the same sin". And he spoke no more.

I replied: "Ciacco, your sorrow weighs
so heavily on me as to bring me to tears;
but do tell if you know, what shall become

of the citizens of that divided city;
whether anyone is just; and what reasons
are behind such discord as assaults her".

And he to me: "after long discordance
blood will be shed, and the rough side
will drive out the other with much offence".

Then it will occur that these will fall
inside three suns, and the other prevail
by the influence of one who brokers.

These will hold power at great length,
weighing the other down heavily,
no matter their cries or offence by it.

The just are two, and not heeded;
Pride, envy and greed are the three
sparks that have ignited all hearts".

Here he ceased his moving remarks.
And I to him: "I still want you to teach
me and gift me more of your words.

Of Farinata and Tegghiaio, so dignified.
Iacopo Rusticucci, Arrigo and Mosca and
others whose minds lent to common good,

Canto VI

say where they are so I may know of them;
for I have pressing need to know whether
Heaven sweetens or hell embitters them".

And he: "they are with most blackened souls;
various sins gravitated them to deeper hell:
if you decline that far, there you'll see them.

But when you return to the sweet world,
I pray you remember me to the living:
no more will I say to you or answer you".

He rolled his eyes and his gaze distorted;
looking at me a little he bowed his head:
crumpling alongside those others blind.

And my Master said: "He will no longer rise
this side of sounding the angelic trumpet,
with the advent of the inimical judge:

each will revisit their own tragic tomb,
take possession of flesh and mortal image,
to hear the eternally reverberating sentence".

Thus we went beyond that putrid mixture
of spirits and of rain, slowly pacing, and
reasoning on and off of life in the future;

so I said: "Master, will this torment
increase following final judgment,
or decrease or stay this scorching?".

And he: "go back to your philosophy,
that asserts: the more perfected a creature,
the more is sensitive to pleasure, so pain too.

Though these cursed people
will never become truly perfected,
more then than now will they be".

We turned along that circular road,
speaking more than which I can re-tell;
arriving at the point of deepening hell:

here we found Pluto, the great enemy.

Canto VII

Here Dante and Virgil arrive at the fourth circle of hell. Virgil reassures Dante and confronts Pluto declaring the mandate to enter that he and Dante have from above. The mere mention of St. Michael the Archangel's victory over the satanic rebellion causes Pluto to collapse where he stands. They enter. Here they see the souls of those guilty of prodigality and of miserliness. Each group is condemned to confront the other repeatedly shouting at each other while pushing boulders with their chests. Reasoning over these they arrive at the river Styx and the fifth circle that contains the wrathful who tear each other to pieces in the mud. Beneath the slimy waterline are the slothful who, submerged, cannot but despair over their wanton lives, their words articulated only by the bubbles that rise to the surface. They arrive at the base of a tower.

"Pape Satàn, pape Satàn aleppe!",
began Pluto with a hoarse voice;
and that noble sage, knowing all,

said to comfort me: "do not let your
fear vex you; as any power he has
won't deny our descent of this ledge".

Then turning to that swollen snout,
he said: "Shut up, damned wolf!
Rot away in your consuming wrath.

Going into the dark is not without reason:
it is willed up above, there where Michael
took revenge on the proud insurrection".

As when sails swollen by the wind
slump in a heap after the mast breaks,
thus to the ground fell the cruel beast.

So we descended into the fourth pit,
proceeding further along the painful slope
that stores all the evil of the universe.

Oh divine justice! who could accumulate
the many unique pains and torments I saw?
and why does our sin deplete us so?

As the waves located above Charybdis,
break against those they collide with,
so here are souls compelled to circle dance.

Here I saw more people than elsewhere,
screaming loudly from both directions
whilst rolling weights using their chests.

Canto VII

They collided; and then and there each
turned round, retracing their steps, crying:
"why tight-fisted?" and "why squander?".

So they returned within the dark circle
from both sides to the opposite points,
yelling the same vile refrain at each other;

once arriving at opposite points, they turned,
in their semicircle toward the other joust.
And I, whose heart was almost pierced,

said: "My master, now do explain to me
who these are, and if all these tonsured
ones to our left were once clerics".

And he to me: "each was so short
sighted during their previous life,
their spending had no measure.

Their barking makes this abundantly clear,
when they land at the circle's two points
where their disparate sins decouple them.

These with no hair on their crowns were
clerics including popes and cardinals,
in whom avarice accentuates entitlement".

And I: "Master, amongst these
I would be sure to know some
tainted with those maladies".

And he: "you conceive a vain thought:
the dissolute life that left them sullied,
now makes recognising them difficult.

Eternally will the two together butt:
from the tomb these will resurrect
fists clenched, those with shorn hair.

Bad giving and bad keeping mean paradise
removed them to be here at loggerheads:
It is as it is, I need not further embellish.

Now my son, you can see the brief sham
wealth is when entrusted to fortune's care,
over which human beings do squabble;

so that all the gold now under the sun
and that ever was, to such weary spirits
could not bring repose even to one".

"My Master", said I, "now tell me also:
this Fortune to which you allude, what is it
that it grips the world's wealth in its claws?"

And he to me: "Oh stupid creatures,
so wounded by so much ignorance!
Now you must digest my take on her.

He whose wisdom surpasses everything,
created the heavens and gave a custodian
so each part doth another part brighten,

distributing light uniformly throughout.
In similar fashion with worldly splendour
He ordained a guide and general minister

to assign vain benefits at the fitting time
from nation to nation and lineage to lineage,
beyond the rigour of the human mind;

Canto VII

so a people prospers as another languishes
according to the judgment that she makes,
hiding as she does as a snake in the grass.

Your wisdom cannot counterpose hers:
as she provides, judges, and prosecutes
in her realm as other monarchs in theirs.

Her variability in change never abates:
necessity forces her to act speedily;
hence why one often faces turns of event.

She is the one often put on the cross
even by those who should laud her,
wrongly vilifying and deprecating her;

but she as blessed one cannot hear this:
as happily joined to other primal beings
turns her sphere revelling in blessedness.

So it is time to descend to greater sorrow;
now each star sets that had risen earlier
when I first saw you; we cannot stay longer".

We crossed the circle to the other bank
above where a bubbling spring spills
into a gully that has been formed by it.

The water was much darker than purple;
and we, accompanying blackened waves,
began to descend a peculiar pathway.

To the swamp called Styx does this
pitiful streamlet lead, once descended
to the foot of that maleficent leaden slope.

And I who was engrossed in watching,
saw mud caked people in that swamp,
all naked, with offended disposition.

These beat each other not just with hands,
but with their heads, and chests and feet,
teeth tearing at each other, piece by piece.

The good Master said: "Son, now see
the spirits of those overcome by ire;
and I also want you to surely believe

that under the water are spirits who sigh,
and cause the water's surface to bubble,
as you can see wherever turns your eye.

Stuck in slurry they say: 'grim were we
in the sweet air enlivened by sun's rays,
carrying within shrouded slothfulness:

now we lie grim in this blackened slime'.
This canticle gurgles within their throats,
as they cannot say it in complete words".

so we turned round that filthy pit in
a large arc between dried bank and bog,
with eyes drawn to those guzzling mud.

In the end, we arrived at the foot of a tower.

Canto VIII

Dante tells us that well prior to arriving at the foot of the tower, his and Virgil's attention came to be directed towards the top of the tower to two flames that communicated with another one in the distance. In querying this with Virgil, it became clear that the flames were a means of communication between the infernal city of Dis and the oarsman, Phlegyas. Upon being signalled, he is called upon to transport damned souls across the river to their infernal sentence. In the case of Dante, Phlegyas attempts to reject the assignment, as Dante is mortal, only to be told he has no choice in the matter as it has already been settled above. With resentful submission, Phlegyas performs his task. During their swift journey, a soul rises from the mud. It is Filippo Argenti who soon resents being remembered with contempt by Dante. Argenti attempts to attack the boat only to be dispensed with by Virgil, who lauds Dante's contempt for him. Ominously, they now turn their attention to hell's city of Dis and its horrific multitude of demonic inhabitants. Virgil attempts to negotiate entry but has the gates unceremoniously slammed in his face. Though guide and pilgrim are perturbed, Divine intervention is about to come in one of the most striking scenes of *Inferno*.

Dante's Inferno

In continuing, I add that much before
we arrived at the foot of that high tower,
our eyes were drawn upwards to its tip

at the two flames that we saw there lit,
to which another flame afar responded,
so distant, you could barely discern it.

And I turned to that font of human intellect;
saying: "What does it say? What responds
the other flame? And who communicates?".

And he: "by casting along the filthy waves
your eye can already see what awaits us,
if the fog of the swamp does not hide it".

A bow string never fired an arrow
that shot through the air so sharply,
as did the small boat which I saw

come towards us across the water,
navigated by merely the one oarsman, that
screamed: "you're seized, maleficent soul!".

"Phlegyas, Phlegyas, your cry rings hollow",
said my Master, "this time: you have us
no more than to cross the muddy swamp".

As one listening to an enormous deception
conducted against him, and is then indignant,
thus Phlegyas became in his pent up anger.

My guide climbed down into the boat,
and drew me to enter after him; and
only when I boarded did it seem laden.

Canto VIII

Immediately the guide and I were on board,
its ancient prow began slicing its way faster
through the water than with others ferried.

While we sailed through the dead channel,
one covered in mud appeared before me,
saying: "who are you here before his time?".

And I: "If I do come, I come not to stay;
but who are you that are so besmeared?".
And he: "You can see I am one crying".

And I to him: "In tears and with wailing,
damned spirit, may you so remain; for I
know you, though you be covered in filth".

At that he extended both hands to the boat;
my Master at the ready shoved him back,
saying: "away with you to the other dogs!".

He then placed his arms around my neck;
kissed my face and said: "Disdaining soul,
blessed was she who conceived thee!

In life this was one who lived arrogantly;
his memory is not enriched by goodness:
hence his soul is here in a state of fury.

How many there see themselves great kings
who will come here and lie in mud as pigs,
leaving contemptible reputation in their wake".

And I: "Master I so very much desire
to see him thrust under in this sauce
before we take our leave of this lake".

And he to me: "before the shore
you will see, you will be satisfied:
it is just you enjoy such a desire".

Shortly after, I witnessed his mutilation
at the hands of the mud caked cohort,
which I still praise and thank God for.

All yelled: "Get Filippo Argenti!"
and that irascible Florentine spirit
tore at himself with his own teeth.

There we left he of whom I no longer speak;
but my ears were struck by a cacophony,
causing my eye to open widely ahead of me.

The good Master said: "now, dear son,
the approaching city has the name Dis,
with crushed citizens, with a great army".

And I: "Master, already its mosques
I see emerge clearly on distant dale,
red as if extracted from a furnace

fire". And he said: "the eternal fire
raging within makes them seem red,
as you behold across this deep hell".

We finally arrived in the deep moats
that surround that inconsolable city:
the walls seeming as if made of iron.

Not without first making a wide traverse,
did we arrive where the oarsman loudly
shouted: "disembark, this is the entrance".

Canto VIII

I saw over a thousand at the gates
having precipitated out of Heaven,
angrily saying: "who is this not dead

travelling the kingdom of the dead?".
And my wise master motioned to them
that he wanted to speak over to one side.

Then their disdain diminished somewhat
saying: "come on your own, he can go
that had the gall to enter this kingdom.

May he return by the road rashly taken:
if able to; indeed you that escorted him
into this dark region, here will remain".

Imagine, reader, how uncomfortable I was
at the sound of those maleficent words,
thinking that I would never return at all.

"Oh my dear guide, who seventy times
seven gave me confidence and extricated
me from the great peril I had to face,

don't leave me", said I, "abandoned thus;
and if our going further on is denied us,
let us rapidly our steps together retrace".

And that Lord who had led me there,
said: "Do not fear; because no one can
deny our access; from such a one giving it.

But wait here, and sustain and comfort
your weary spirit on good hope, as I
will not leave you in this deep world".

So my sweet father left, abandoning
me here on my own in doubt, torn
between the yes and no of my mind.

I could not hear what was addressed;
but he hadn't stayed there very long,
when each raced back behind its walls.

Our adversaries then shut those gates
in my master's face, who, left outside,
turned back to me at protracted pace.

He was downcast and crestfallen having
lost his confidence, sighing and saying:
"Who has denied me the home of sorrow!".

And he said: "for all the anger I have,
don't lose heart, as I will pass the test,
whatever exclusion is conjured within.

This their presumptuousness is not new;
as was used already at a less hidden gate,
which unlocked still remains that way.

Above it you saw that deathly inscription:
and now already through it is descending,
traversing the circles not needing a guide,

one for whom the domain shall open".

Canto IX

The impact of the demonic aggression against Virgil and anticipation of the coming Divine intervention continue in this Canto. Dante is terrified and Virgil perturbed, as the latter alternates between perplexity at the delay and conviction that help would come. Dante queries whether anyone has ever exited from the circles of hell. Virgil recounts the story of how the sorceress Erichtho summoned his shade to go down to deepest hell and bring her up a traitor. So Virgil knows the path well. The travellers at this point witness the appearance of three horrifying furies at the top of the tower. These, the Erinyes, cry out to Medusa so Dante can be turned to stone. Virgil causes Dante to cover his eyes and for good measure adds his hands over Dante's as such an event would prevent Dante ever exiting inferno. At the peak of the infernal drama that threatens Dante's destruction, a greater violence unleashes itself across the river Styx, driving over a thousand souls before it. The Divine emissary has arrived.

My facial pallor painted by cowardice
upon seeing my guide turning back,
made him restrain his change of colour.

He stood still, as attentive man listening;
for he could not see far into the distance
through black air and through dense fog.

"Yet we will win the battle", he began,
"unless…but such help was promised.
Oh how tardy is that other to arrive!"

I saw well how he overrode that which
he began to say with what he then said,
in later words quite different to the first;

nevertheless his words engendered fear,
because I heard the shift in sentence
have meaning worse than was meant.

"Has this lower circle of the infernal chasm
ever had someone from the first circle,
where punishment is only of hope dashed?".

I put this question and he replied,
"rarely does it happen that any of
us takes this path on which I travel.

It is true that I was here once before,
conjured by cruel sorceress Erichtho
who called spirits back to their bodies.

Only but recently had I shed my flesh,
when she caused me to enter these walls,
to evoke a spirit from the circle of Judas.

Canto IX

That is the deepest and darkest of places,
most distant from the Heaven turning all:
I know the path well; so rest ye assured.

This swamp giving off the offensive odour
does circumscribe the afflicted city, into
which we cannot now enter without anger".

He added more, but it doesn't come to mind;
as my eye was completely drawn towards
that high tower with its scorching summit,

wherein immediately rose erect
three infernal furies stained in blood,
bearing female physique and gesture,

waists girded by bright green hydras;
their hair being fine snakes and vipers
covering around the ferocious temples.

And he, familiar with the handmaids
of the queen of eternal wailing,
said: "Look, the ferocious Erinyes!

This one that is to the left is Megaera;
she that is crying to the right is Alecto;
Tisiphone is at the centre"; and he went silent.

Each lacerated its chest with its talons;
palms striking 'selves and screeching so
loudly, that in fear I held onto the poet.

"Come Medusa let's turn him to stone",
they were all saying while looking down:
"wrongly did we not avenge Theseus' assault".

Dante's Inferno

"Turn around and shut your eyes for if the
Gorgon appears and you should see her,
there will be no hope of your return above".

So said my Master; and he himself turned me
around, not content with my hands covering
my eyes he added his to help cover them.

Oh you who have integrity of intellect,
focus your eye on the hidden doctrine
under the veil of the mysterious verses.

Immediately across the murky waves
came a fracas of sound, full of terror,
causing both banks of hell to rumble,

no different is it to when a wind
launched by contrasting temperature,
strikes at a forest and with no restraint

breaks, crushes and drags away branches;
proceeding proudly in the driven dust,
frightening away animals and shepherds.

He released my eyes and said: "now focus
your gaze upon that ancient quagmire
where the dark fog at its densest hangs".

Just as frogs facing their enemy water
snake, all disperse through the pond
until each lays itself flat along the bed,

saw I more than a thousand devastated souls
flee the same way before one whose feet
hovered on the Styx while remaining dry.

Canto IX

Pushing greasy vapours from his face,
he was waving his left hand regularly;
seemingly discomforted only by this.

I surely realised he was a celestial emissary,
and turned to my master; who motioned
I be quiet and bow before such an envoy.

Oh how full of disdain he appeared to me!
Coming to the gate and with a small wand
opening it, there being nothing to resist it.

"Oh exiles from Heaven, despised mob",
he began upon that horrific threshold,
"wherefrom has such arrogance arisen?

Why do you recalcitrate against that will
whose outcome can never be truncated,
and has many times your pain augmented?

What does it serve you to clash with fate?
Your Cerberus, if you recall, still bears flayed
chin and throat as consequences to this day".

He then turned back on the sullied path,
without word in our direction, but was as
man seized and driven by a preoccupation

other than those set out there before him:
and we set foot forward toward that city,
secure in those holy words he had uttered.

We entered without any opposition;
and I, who had the desire to examine
the nature of what such fortress enclosed,

Dante's Inferno

gazed around as soon as I had entered:
and saw a great plain in every direction,
full of sorrow and of terrible torment.

Just as at Arli, where the Rhone becomes
marshland and Pola, near the Kvarner Gulf
at the door to Italy and her border bathes,

the tombs do variegate all of the terrain,
so too here they were in every direction,
except this design held far bitterer pain;

for flames were interspersed between tombs
by which they glowed much while scorched,
hotter than any iron requires to be wrought.

All of them had lids that were kept open
from which came such intense lamentation,
clearly telling of the despaired and tortured.

And I: "Master, who are these people
that, buried under those stone tombs,
can be heard sighing so sorrowfully?".

And he to me: "Here lie the Heresiarchs
with their disciples of every sect; many
more than you can imagine fill the tombs.

Like is buried with like in here, and
tombs are at higher or lower heat".
And after he turned right, we walked

between torments and high fortifications.

Canto X

As Dante and Virgil venture forth among the tombs of the heretics, Dante queries whether they can meet those buried there. As Virgil confirms in the affirmative, a voice emanates from a tomb declaring recognition of Dante's Florentine pronunciation in its courtesy. The voice of a once political enemy, Farinata, also declares how injurious he had been in participating in the reprisal against the Guelfs for ejecting his party, the Ghibellines, from Florence in 1258. As Dante looks on and with Virgil's prompting, he sees the large figure of Farinata rise up out of the tomb with imperious demeanour, even towards the hell that surrounds him. Dante and Farinata contrast ideological and familial alliances, when they are interrupted by another entombed soul, Guido Cavalcanti, who is enquiring about whether his son is still alive. Dante hesitates in responding and that is interpreted by Cavalcanti as implying that he has died, at which Cavalcanti collapses. Without batting an eyelid, Farinata resumes the conversation and while discussing the respective exiles of the parties, prophesies that Dante too will know the burden of that experience. Farinata then answers Dante's question as to why the dead can see into the future but do not know the present, adding what will happen to those faculties at the Last Judgment.

Now proceeding on a concealed path
between the city walls and torments,
was my Master leading and I pursuing.

"Oh sublime virtue, that by the impious circles
lead me" I began, "in whichever way you wish,
do talk to me and satisfy these my desires.

As for these damned that lie in tombs,
could we see them? Given the lids are
open and no-one else is guarding them".

And he to me: "they will all be sealed upon
the souls' return from the valley of Jehoshaphat
carrying the bodies that they left up there.

Those whose burial place is here are
along with Epicurus all his disciples,
who claim the soul with the body dies.

Therefore as for the question you ask
it will quickly be satisfied within here;
as will that wish you keep quiet about".

And I: "Good guide, I do not withhold
from you except so as to speak reservedly,
as you have encouraged not just now".

"Oh Tuscan who through this infernal city
as a mortal are speaking with such dignity,
may it please you to sojourn over here.

Your articulation doth manifest
your birth in that noble homeland,
to which I was though, too violent".

Canto X

This voice sprang all of a sudden
from one of the tombs; so I shifted,
nervously, a bit closer to my guide.

He said: "Turn! What are you doing?
Look at Farinata who has straightened:
You can see him entirely from waste up".

I had already fixed my eyes upon his face;
and he rising held his chest and forehead
as if all hell were utterly beneath him.

And my guide's capable and ready hands
pushed me to him among the sepulchres,
saying: "Now be measured in your words".

As soon as I stood at the foot of the tomb,
he glanced at me, and, nearly disdainfully,
he then asked: "What is your ancestry?".

I who was anxious to obey,
did not hold back but opened up fully;
at which he raised his eyebrows slightly;

then he said: "they were a bitter enemy
of mine and my forefathers and my party,
so that two times I dispensed with them'.

"If expelled, they returned from everywhere",
I answered, "on first and second occasion; but
your ancestors did not well acquire that art".

Just then at the tomb opening rose
a spirit up to his chin alongside him:
I think he had gotten on his knees.

Dante's Inferno

He looked around me, as if hoping to
see some other person there with me;
and when his speculation had dissipated,

crying he said: "if it is high intellect by
which you move through this dismal gaol,
where is my son? And why not with you?"

And I to him: "I am not here on my own:
he in attendance there guides me through;
he who perhaps your Guido held in contempt".

His words and his type of punishment
had told me already what his name was;
hence why my answer was so complete.

Suddenly straightening he yelled: "What?
Did you say "he *held*"? Is he not still alive?
Does not sweet sunlight still strike his eyes?".

When he noticed some hesitation
from me in answering the question,
he fell flat on his back away from view.

But that majestic spirit, at whose invitation
I had paused, remained unaffected, not
moving his head, nor bending sideways;

and continuing his line of conversation,
he said, "if they badly acquired that art,
such torments me more than this bed.

But not even fifty lunar cycles shall ignite
the face of the noblewoman reigning here,
before you know the weight of that art.

Canto X

And may you return to the sweet world,
tell me: why are your people so cruel
against mine within each legal rule?".

And I: "the carnage and massive slaughter
that turned red the Arbia's waters,
leads us to such prayer in our senate".

Then after having shaken his head sighing,
he said, "I wasn't alone in that nor certainly
was without reason in joining the others.

But it was only I, when all had accepted
that Florence should be done away with,
who stood up and openly her defended".

"Oh, I pray your descendants will find peace",
I implored: "please resolve this question
that has confused my capacity to reason.

It seems you all see, if I hear correctly,
in advance what the future does carry,
but the present do view differently".

"We see, as those who are vision impaired,"
he said, "those things that are far away;
such as still shined on by the King of kings.

When they approach or occur, all is absent
from our minds; and if others tell us not,
we know nothing of your human condition.

Therefore you will infer that our knowledge
will come to its final end from that point
at which the door to the future closes".

Then, regretful of my previous error,
I said: "now will you tell that fallen one
that his son is still amongst the living;

and that if I earlier hesitated to answer,
let him know that I did so as I wrestled
with the difficulty you have now resolved".

And just then my Master was calling me;
so I prayed the spirit would more hurriedly
tell me who his companions were in there.

He replied: "I lie with over one thousand:
here are the second Federick and the Cardinal;
and as for the others I shall remain silent".

He then hid; and towards the great
poet I turned my steps, thinking over
those words that seemed threatening.

He moved; and then while we walked
he asked: "why are you so perturbed?".
And I answered his request completely.

"Your mind must remember that prophecy
you heard against you", the sage commanded;
"now mark my words", raising his finger:

"when you come before the warm light
of she whose magnificent eyes see all,
from her you will know your life's path".

Then he moved his feet to the left:
we headed from the wall to the centre
along a path that opens to a valley,

whose stench disgusted even so high up.

Canto XI

The two continue their journey through the sixth circle and find themselves overwhelmed by the terrible stench rising from the pit. It is so overpowering that they must stop to withstand and become accustomed to it. They do so behind the lid of the large tomb of Pope Anastasius. As Dante wants to make the most of the opportunity to converse, Virgil proceeds to explain the intricacies of the degree and manner of punishment that souls are subjected to in Inferno. He does so in terms of sinful cause and horrific effect.

At the outer ledge of a high embankment
made by a circle of large fractured rocks,
we came over the more cruelly crammed:

and there, due to the awful overspill
of stench the deep abyss eructates,
we sought refuge behind a coffin lid

of a large tomb, where I read the inscription
that said: "Here lies Pope Anastasius,
led from the straight path by Photinus".

"We should delay our descent a bit,
that our sense of smell may adapt
to the stench; so later won't detect it",

So said the Master; and I: "Can you
find compensation so we don't waste
time". And he: "my thoughts exactly".

"My son, within these rocks", he began,
"are three circles one aligned below
the other, like the ones you left above.

They are all full of accursed spirits;
but so you later understand at first sight,
listen to the how and why they so unite.

All maliciousness, which Heaven detests,
aims at injustice, and it is always attained
by either force or fraud offending another.

And as fraud is that sin exclusive to man,
it displeases God more; so deeper down
lie the fraudulent, and more pain assails them.

Canto XI

The first circle is filled with the violent;
and as violence inflicts on three persons,
in three circular levels is divided and built.

Force attacks God, self and neighbour,
and the latter: they or their possessions,
as you'll hear my reasoning make clearer.

Death by force and grave injury is visited
upon neighbour, and as to his property:
destruction, arson and violent stealing;

So assassins and the unlawfully violent,
arsonists and bandits, are each tormented
in measured manner in the first ring.

Man can turn a violent hand against self
and his goods; therefore it is the second
ring wherein he must repent fruitlessly

whoever deprives your world of his life,
or squanders their money by gambling,
and cries there instead of being happy.

It is possible to be violent to the Deity,
denying it in your heart and cursing it,
and despising nature and her generosity;

and therefore the smallest ring stamps its
seal on Sodom and Cahors and those who,
despising God in their hearts, blaspheme.

Fraud, that chews away every conscience,
can be used towards they that trust you
and those who have not invested in trust.

This second way seems to cleave
only the bond of love from nature;
so, in the second circle do nest

hypocrisy, flattery, sorcery,
falseness, stealing, simony,
panderers, swindlers and like foulness.

By other fraud is love forgotten
begotten of nature, which then,
by faith leads to the birth of trust;

so in the smaller circle which is the centre
of the universe and Dis's foundation stone,
each and every traitor is consumed eternally".

And I: "Master, your reasoning proceeds
most clearly, and well describes this
chasm's features and its occupants.

But tell me: why those of the muddy
swamp that wind buffets and rain beats,
and they who with sharp tongues collide,

are they not punished within the flaming
hot city, if God's contempt is upon them?
and if it is not, why are they castigated so?".

And he "why such distraction", adding,
"from your mind's usual course? Or what
other direction are your thoughts aimed at?

Do you not remember those words
by which your reading of Ethics treats
the three categories Heaven disdains,

Canto XI

wantonness, malice and insane
bestiality? And how wantonness
offending God less, attracts less blame?

If you consider deeply this doctrine,
and bring to mind who they are that
outside and above us suffer pain,

you will well see why they are separated
from these evil ones, and why a less angry
divine retribution hammers them so".

"Oh you sun that heals all blurred vision,
you so satisfy when you resolve questions,
even doubt itself has solution's pleasure.

Now if you make your way back a little",
said I, "to when you said usury offends
Divine goodness; and resolve my question".

"Philosophy", he said, "for who understands,
says clearly, and not just in one place,
how nature follows its own course

from the Divine wisdom and its art;
and if you recollect well your Physics,
you will find, not too many pages in,

that human art when it evolves as enabled,
follows nature as disciple follows master;
so your art is almost God's grandchild.

So from this duality, if you call to mind
the beginning of Genesis, people must
draw their sustenance and make progress;

and since the usurer travels another path,
he detests both nature and its disciple art,
as he places his hope in something other.

But follow me now, for it is time to go;
as the Fish are glistening on the horizon,
and the Wain is precisely over Caurus,

and further on we will descend this bank".

Canto XII

Dante and Virgil approach the slope leading to the seventh circle. The structure of the slope is derived from a massive landslide created when, following His death, Jesus descended into hell with the cataclysmic implication of his dominance over death resulting in the resurrection. At its edge, the abyss has the half human half beast Minotaur, that oversees the damned for the sin of violence. This includes violence against Nature itself in the form of the sin of bestiality resulting in its half human half beast offspring. Following the challenge from Virgil, the Minotaur's convulsive fit is so great that it overwhelms him, giving guide and pilgrim the opportunity to bypass it while it is in the throes of convulsion. Having descended into the abyss, they approach the river of boiling blood in which are immersed the violent to a requisite depth. They are maintained at their depth by the many circling centaurs who fire arrows at souls attempting to surface to relieve their agony. Virgil approaches the lead centaurs managing to enlist a guide, Nessus, who leads them along the circle, pointing out various damned souls and the history that condemns them.

We then reached a point of descent
so steep, and he reclining there was
such, that all eyes would be repelled.

Like that landslide that struck the river-
bed of the Adige on this side of Trent,
caused by earthquake or by erosion,

from the mountain top where it came,
to the plain below, stone so shattered,
it provided a pathway to those above:

so too was as steep that descent;
and at the very edge of the precipice
lay stretched out the infamy of Crete

that was conceived in the fake cow;
and when he saw us, he bit himself,
like one ruptured within by anger.

My sage shouted at him: "Perhaps
you think this is the Duke of Athens,
bringing you death while up on earth?

Away, beast, he has not come
under your sister's instructions,
rather to see your punishments".

In the same way a bull breaks its straps
having already received the mortal blow,
and cannot run, but tosses this way and that,

so too did I see the Minotaur react; and
the alert one yelled: "run to the opening;
best you descend as it is gripped by rage".

Canto XII

So we took the path down the ravine
of those rocks, often shifting underfoot
on account of bearing unusual weight.

I was pensive; and he: "You're thinking
perhaps of this rocky debris, guarded
by the monstrous fury I just extinguished.

I want you to know the other time
I descended here into deeper hell,
that this rock did not as yet fall.

If memory serves me well, it was just prior
to the arrival of He who took the great
booty from Dis in the first circle,

the fetid abyss so shook to its very
foundation, that I thought the universe
was taken by the love, some believe

more than once converted the world to chaos;
and it was at that moment this old rock,
collapsed broken, here and elsewhere.

But look carefully at the valley, as
nears the river of blood in which boil
any who harm others with violence".

Oh blind avarice and crazed anger,
that spur us on in life's brief span,
and eternally immerses us so badly!

I saw a large moat shaped as an arc,
its form embracing the whole plain,
just as my guide had earlier told me;

and between it and the bank, in single file
galloped centaurs, armed with arrows,
in the same way as they hunted on earth.

Seeing us come down, they all stopped,
and from the host there detached three
with bows and finest arrows at the ready;

one yelled from afar: "To which punishment
come you who do now descend the slope?
Say so right there; or I will draw my bow".

My Master then replied: "we will answer
Chiron when we have come closer there:
your haste has always been your failing".

Then he held me, saying: "That is Nessus,
who died for love of beautiful Deianira,
and later avenged himself, against self.

And the middle one with his face down,
is great Chiron, who brought up Achilles;
the other Pholus, who was so full of anger.

In thousands they rotate round the pit,
firing arrows at any spirit that raises it-
self above the blood level of its guilt".

We approached those fleet footed beasts:
Chiron took an arrow, using the nock
to push his beard back along his jaw.

After he had uncovered his large mouth,
he said to his companions "Did you notice the
the rear one shifts whatever he touches?

Canto XII

Dead men's feet do not do this".
And my good guide already at his chest,
where the dual natures are conjoined,

replied: "he is indeed alive, to he
thus alone must I show the dark valley;
necessity spurns us, not enjoyment.

One came leaving her hallelujah
and delegated me this new office:
he is not a thief, neither am I one.

But in name of the virtue by which I take
steps along such a fierce road as this,
grant one of your group accompany us,

and can show us where a ford is,
and would carry him on his back,
as he is not spirit moving in the air".

Chiron turned around to his right breast,
and to Nessus: "Return and guide them,
and drive away any team hindering you".

So we moved on entrusted to the escort
along the shore of the boiling vermillion,
where those that boiled, loudly shrieked.

I saw souls immersed up to the eyelashes;
and the great centaur said: "these are
tyrants who shed blood and did plunder.

Here they cry for their merciless offences;
here is Alexander, and ferocious Dionysius
who imposed on Sicily years of anguish.

Dante's Inferno

And that forehead with such black hair
is Azzolino; and that other who is blond,
is Opizzo from the East who was indeed

killed by his adopted son up on earth".
I then turned to the poet and he said:
"he will now guide first, and I second".

Shortly after the centaur halted above
some spirits immersed to their throats
seeming to emerge from the hot spring.

He pointed out a shadow left to one side,
saying: "This one knifed in God's bosom
that heart still dripping onto the Thames".

I then saw people holding their heads
and their chests above the bloody river;
and recognised many of them there.

Then little by little the level of blood
lowered, so it cooked only their feet;
and we made our way across the ford.

"As you can see from over here the
bloody spring level gradually drops".
said the centaur, "I want you to know

that the other side's bed increases
in depth bit by bit, until it reaches
where tyrants do collect to moan.

Divine justice on this side stings
Attila, divine whip hand on earth,
Pyrrhus and Sextus; ever milking

the tears, drawn out by the boiling,
of Rinier da Corneto, Rinier Pazzo,
who waged war as highwaymen".

So he turned and crossed the ford again.

Canto XIII

The centaur Nessus has barely led the poets across the Phlegethon, when they instantly find themselves in a thick forest of ominously gnarled, dark and prickled undergrowth. It is the realm of the harpies, creatures who are part woman and part bird. The bestial theme of the previous Canto continues with these who nest in the forest and torment its inhabitant souls. The metamorphosis perversely extends to the rendering of souls into a hideous vegetable form. It is the reductionist state of those sentenced by Minos due to the sin of self-violence to the point of immobility and vulnerability to hell's predatory torturers. The vulnerability is introduced to the reader by Virgil inviting Dante to snap a twig, which immediately remonstrates at the act.[1] It becomes enhanced by the impact of two souls in naked human form[2] attempting to escape a pack of wild dogs. The vegetation is thrashed causing incalculable pain until the dogs catch their prey and proceed to dismember them, carrying off the torn flesh in their jaws. The gratuitousness of violence aligns as a metaphor for the senselessness and intensity of the sin that has remained unrepented of. The savagery ends with Virgil inviting one of the devasted, lamenting bushes to declare who he was while on earth. The answer came that he was a Florentine who took his own life by hanging himself in his home.

---

1. The soul is that of *Pier delle Vigne*, advisor to Frederick II of Sicily and who because of his falling out of favour took his own life.
2. *Lano da Siena* and *Giacomo da Sant'Andrea*.

Nessus had not yet made the crossing,
when we found our way into a wood
which was not marked by any path.

The leaves were not green but blackened;
no flowing branches just knots and twists;
no fruit was there, but only toxic prickles.

Wild animals who detest cultivated land
between Cecina and Corneto have no such
bristling prickle bush nor dense scrubland.

It is here the ugly harpies build their nests,
who expelled the Trojans from Strophades
lugubriously prophesising future tragedies.

Having wide wings, human necks and faces,
clawed hooves, feathered large bellies;
they screech freakish laments from the trees.

And the good Master began saying to me:
"Before going any further, know you are
in the second ring and here will remain

until arriving on the horrific sandy plain.
Hence be on your guard; as you will see
what wouldn't be believed if I described".

I could hear howls from every direction
but could not see anyone emitting them;
at which I came to a halt, all perplexed.

I thought he thought that I was thinking
all voices emanating from that boscage
were spirits hiding themselves from us.

Canto XIII

Therefore the Master said: "If you break
an odd twig of one of these here plants,
the thoughts you are having will cease".

So I extended my hand a little forward
and picked a twig of a large prickle bush;
and its trunk screamed: "Why snap me?".

After then having oozed some black blood,
it started again: "Why do you tear at me?
Have you no sense of pity whatsoever?

We were once men, and are now bushes:
surely you could have been more piteous,
even if we had been the spirits of snakes".

Like when green wood is burning up at
one end, and from the other bleeds sap
whistling from the air escaping from it,

so from the broken twig poured together
words and blood; at which I let the branch
drop, and stood as a man taken by fear.

"If he had been able to believe earlier",
replied my sage, "oh harmed soul,
what he had seen only in my verses,

he wouldn't have raised a hand against you;
but your unbelievable state led me to induce
him to do what weighs heavily upon me.

But tell him who you once were, so to
remediate this he may restore your fame
up on earth, where his return is secured".

And the trunk: "Sweetly your words entice,
so I cannot be silent; and may I not burden
if tempted to converse with you a touch.

I am the confidant who held both keys to
Frederick's heart, and who turned them,
locking and unlocking, oh so exquisitely,

that I kept nearly all men from his secrets;
I brought such fidelity to that high office,
that it cost me my sleep and my very life.

The harlot that never withheld a
wanton eye from Caesar's house,
common death and vice of courts,

inflaming sentiments of all against me;
did the inflamed so inflame Augustus,
that joyful honours turned to sad grief.

My spirit, driven by disdainful feeling,
sought death to escape disdain of me,
making me unjust against my just self.

By the newly grown roots of this bush
I swear that I never did once betray
my lord, who was so worthy of honour.

And if any of you return to the world,
restore my reputation, that lies over-
whelmed by the blow envy struck".

The poet, pausing momentarily then said:
"As he is quiet do not lose opportunity;
but speak and ask him whatever you like".

Canto XIII

So I said: "You enquire further of him
about what you think would satisfy me;
for I could not, as my heart's full of pity".

So he began: "So this man may freely
do what your words now ask of him,
incarcerated spirit, may it please you

to elaborate on how souls become infused
in these gnarls; and tell us, if you are able,
if anyone was ever freed from such limbs".

Then the trunk heaved a heavy breath,
and so that wind became these words:
"You will be answered very briefly.

When the savage soul separates itself
from the body it tears itself away from,
Minos sends it into the seventh abyss.

It falls in bushland, not preordained place;
but anywhere that luck would have it,
and there sprouts as does a spelt seed,

emerging as a sapling, then as a wild bush:
Harpies, inflicting pain while feeding off
leaves, give to pain its window of escape.

As others we will return to claim our bodies,
but not for which to then clothe ourselves,
as it is unjust to reclaim what one discards.

We will drag them here, in this forest
of doom our bodies will be hung, each
on the prickle bush of its inimical soul".

Dante's Inferno

We were still attentive to the trunk,
thinking it would add further words,
when we were startled by a sound,

similarly to he that hears the coming
boar being hunted down, hearing the
noise of dogs and thrashing branches,

suddenly to the left appeared two spirits,
naked and lacerated, bolting in such force,
as to smash through every prickle branch.

The one ahead: "death, come, come!".
The other, aware he was lagging behind,
cried, "Lano there was no such agility

in your legs at the jousting at Toppo!".
And then perhaps for breathlessness,
he hid enveloping himself inside a bush.

The forest behind them was full
of black, voracious, agile she-dogs
like hunting dogs just unchained.

They sank their teeth into the one hiding,
and shredded him piece by piece; then
carried away each of the agonised limbs.

Then my guide took me by the hand,
and drew me to that bush now crying
in vain via broken, bleeding branches.

"Oh Giacomo", he said, "of Sant'Andrea,
how did it avail to use me as a shield?
why am I to blame for your evil life?".

Canto XIII

When Master stopped over him, he said:
"Who were you, that of so many points
exhale such doleful, bloodied discourse?".

And he to us: "oh spirits that have come
in time to see the indecorous laceration
that has so torn all my fronds from me,

gather them from beneath my sad bush.
I was of the city its first patron replaced
with the Baptist; so for this the first one

will always sadden her with his art of war;
and thankfully a semblance of him still
remains on the bridge crossing the Arno,

otherwise the citizens that rebuilt her
on the ashes that Attila left behind,
would all have laboured for naught.

I turned my house into my scaffold".

Canto XIV

Dante, out of compassionate patriotism, complies with the anonymous Florentine's request to gather up his dispersed remnants. He and Virgil then arrive at the outer edge of the circle to observe the horror of a barren, sandy landscape. It is designed for eternal retribution against those who died in a sinful state of blasphemy, usury or sodomy, respectively. Virgil explains that those who are prostrate are the blasphemers, those crouched the usurers and those constantly in motion, the sodomites. Upon them fall sheets of flames that torment unrelentingly. They also fall on the sand and ignite it, so the souls are in a perpetual state of fruitlessly attempting to doubly avoid and flick away the burning sensations. The travellers interact with Capaneus whose contempt for God and his fury, Virgil tells him, are the very source of the intensity of his punishment. Finally, in answering Dante's question about the source of the rivers in hell, Virgil describes the Old Man of Crete. In intricate metaphorical expression, Virgil explains it is from his tears that all rivers in hell are sourced.

Dante's Inferno

Since patriotism for my birthplace moved
me to, I did collect the dispersed leaves
giving them to he whose voice had waned.

So we arrived at the perimeter where the
second ring leads to the third, wherein
the horrific expression of justice is seen.

To best depict these things unknown,
I say that we arrived at a desolate plain
that allows no vegetation on its terrain.

The sorrowful forest girds all around it,
as bloody river doth enclose the forest;
hereat we stopped at its absolute limit.

The ground was of dense and arid sand
no different to the other place that had
once under Cato's feet been trampled.

Oh retribution of God, how you should
be feared by each who reads about what
manifested itself before my very eyes!

I saw many flocks of naked souls
all crying most miserably, each
subject to a law unique to them.

Some of them were flat on their backs,
some others sat there tightly curled up,
and others still were pacing continually.

Those pacing were the most in number,
while those lying in torment were fewer,
but their lamenting tongues were looser.

Canto XIV

Across all the sandy landscape were
raining softly falling sheets of flame,
as alpine snow when the wind is still.

Which Alexander saw in the scorching
parts of India fall upon his military,
retaining their form till fallen to earth,

for which ordered earth be stamped
by his army, so each flame would be
extinguished whilst still a single flame:

in this way did fall the eternal flames;
causing sand to catch fire, as from tinder
meeting flint, so as to double the dolour.

There was no repose in the dance of
damned hands shaking this way and
that, flicking away each new flame.

I began: "Master, you who vanquish
all things except those indurated devils
who came at us at the entrance gate,

who is that stately one seemingly untouched
by flames, reclining spiteful and disdainful
so it seems the rain cannot martyrise him?".

And that very same soul, who noticed
that I was asking my guide about him,
screamed: "As in life, so am I in death.

May Jove exhaust his monger from whom
angrily grabbed the acute lightening bolt
with which he struck me the day I died;

and one after another, he tire others
at the blackened forge in Mongibello,
while crying 'Expert Vulcan, help, help!',

the same way as at the battle of Phlegra,
strike me with full force of his lightning:
but without the joyful revenge from it".

Then my guide spoke with such power,
that I had never heard him so loud:
"Oh Capaneus, as your pride remains

indomitable, so the more you are
punished; no torment, other than
your very ire, best suits your fury".

he then turned to me with placid face,
saying: "He was one of the seven kings
besieging Thebes; and held and seemingly

holds God in disdain, and of little value;
but, as I did so tell him, his spitefulness
is fittingly ornamented upon his chest.

Now follow me, and still be careful not
to place your feet on the burning sand;
but to keep them at the wooded edge".

We arrived without talking to where
out of bushland flows a small stream,
the redness of which still terrifies me.

As the stream issuing from the Bulicame
that sinful women share between them,
so this one makes its way across the sand.

Canto XIV

Its bed and both of the banks were made
of stone, as were the margins either side:
therefore I recognised this was our path.

"In everything else I've shown you,
after having entered the doorway
whose ingress is denied to no-one,

there is nothing your eyes have seen
as substantive as this river before us,
that puts out all the flames above it".

These were Master's words; so
I prayed he grant me the food
he had made me so hungry for.

"In the middle of the sea is a place of ruin",
he then began, "that is called Crete, under
whose king the world was once chaste.

There is a mountain there once a delight
for its streams and vegetation, named Ida;
now forsaken as a thing old and in tatters.

Rhea chose it as secure cradle for her infant
son, and to better hide him when he cried,
she made it that others loudly screamed.

Within the mountain rises a great old man,
whose shoulders keeps towards Damietta
and looks on Rome as if it were a mirror.

His head is formed of finest gold,
His arms and chest of pure silver,
then brass to where his legs bifurcate;

from there down he is all select iron,
except for his right foot made of clay,
he leaning more on it than the other.

Each part except the gold, is fractured
and through the fissure sheds tears,
that, collected, corrode the cavern.

They traverse rock to rock to this valley;
forming Acheron, Styx, and Phlegethon;
then descending down this narrow canal;

finally, when they can no longer descend,
they form Cocytus; and what that pond is
I will not discuss, you can see for yourself".

And I to him: "if this streamlet
therefore has source on our world,
why does it just show at this edge?".

And he: "you know this place is circular;
and although you have come a long way,
descending to your left towards the base,

you are yet to travel all the perimeter;
so if a new thing should to us appear,
you needn't display such astonishment".

And I further: "Master, where are Lethe
and Phlegethon? You are silent on the one,
yet say the other is from this rain of tears".

"I certainly like all the questions you ask",
he replied, "but the boiling of red water
should surely resolve one of your doubts.

Canto XIV

You'll see Lethe, but outside this cavern,
where spirits go wash themselves clean
when the repented of sin is remitted".

Then he said: "Now is time to distance our-
selves from the forest, ensure you follow me:
the margins are our path as will not burn,

and above them, each flame extinguishes".

Canto XV

The travellers proceed through the sandy plain by walking along the edge of the canal. They are a long distance from the forest now when they come upon men who scrutinise them from head to toe. One of them is Brunetto Latini, distinguished Florentine intellectual whom Dante treats with the utmost respect. This is evident in his use of the deferential pronoun 'voi' of a subordinate, while Latini uses the familiar form 'tu', indicating seniority. Dante lauds Latini, each expressing support for the other that had been terminated by Latini's death. The deeply personal mutual affection is in stark contrast to the horrid environment surrounding them; Latini having been condemned with the other sodomites he identifies to Dante. The elevated tone of their reunion is cut short by the pending arrival of another group with whom *Ser Brunetto* must not associate. At that, he sprints off to join his troop again. Dante's description of him as an athlete is replete with admiration and affection, describing him as winner of Verona's *Palio del drappo verde*.

Dante's Inferno

Now one of the margins carries us on it;
and the river vapour in casting a shadow,
protects water and banks from the fire.

As Flemish between Wissant and Bruges,
fearing the dashing of waters against them,
erect barriers so that the sea retreats;

as do the Paduans along the Brenta,
to protect their cities and castles,
before Chiarentana feels the heat:

thus were these embankments,
though they were built neither as
high nor solid, by whomever did so.

We were now so far from the forest
to a point I could not have seen it,
even if I had turned back to look,

when we ran into a group of spirits
coming along the bank, and each
was scanning us as during the night

under a new moon one scrutinises
another; and squinted at us as does
the old tailor at the eye of a needle.

While looked up and down by that host,
I was recognised by one, who took
my hem exclaiming: "What a surprise!".

And I, when he extended his arm to me
fixed my gaze upon his singed countenance,
so that his seared face could not prevent

Canto XV

my mind recalling him; and inclining
my hand towards his face, I replied:
"is it really you here, Ser Brunetto?".

And he: "Oh my son, don't be displeased
if Brunetto Latini falls back a bit with you
and leaves the file of others to proceed".

And I to him: "I beg you to with my all;
and if you wish me to sit with you,
I will, if it pleases the one I go with".

"Oh son", he said, "anyone, in this drove
pausing a bit, must lie down a hundred years
without swiping when the fire hurts.

So proceed further: I will follow you;
and I will then re-join my platoon,
that goes weeping its eternal loss".

I did not dare descend from the embankment
to walk level to him; but went head bowed
as a man proceeding with due deference.

He began: "What fortune or destiny
brings you here before your last day?
and who is this showing you the way?".

"Up there above us, in the serene life",
I answered, "I came adrift in a valley,
before arriving at the fullness of age.

Just yesterday morning after I left it:
he appeared, while I turned towards it,
and he leads me home by this pathway".

And he said: "if you follow your star,
you can't fail arriving at a glorious port,
if I judged correctly in the lovely life;

and if I had not died before my time,
seeing Heaven so inclined toward you,
I would have supported your work.

But that ingrate and malign people
descended from ancient Fiesole,
rustic as its mount and livid rock,

will, for your doing right, become your
enemies; since bitter fruit cannot stand
that a sweet fig tree should bear fruit.

Old reputation regards them as blind;
a greedy people, jealous and arrogant:
ensure you're immune to their customs.

Your fortune conserves you much honour,
so one faction and other will hunger for you;
but too distant is the grass from the goat.

May the Fiesolan beasts forage upon
each other, and not touch the plant,
if one still grows upon their manure,

in which resurges the holy seed
of the Romans that remained
when the nest of such iniquity formed".

"If all my wishes had been fulfilled",
I replied, "you would not as yet
have been driven from humanity;

Canto XV

as what is fixed in my mind, now heart-,
felt is the dear and good paternal image
of you on earth when time and again you

taught me how man is eternalised: and
how grateful I am will, for as long as I
live be expressed in my testimony.

I note what you say of my life's course,
and will keep it with other script for a lady
of knowledge to interpret, if I reach her.

I just want it to be evident to you,
but for conscience rebuking me,
I accept what Fortune has in store.

Such a bond is not new to my ear;
so may Fortune turn her wheel as she
pleases, and the peasant turn his hoe".

My Master then turning to his right
looked back at me, saying: "Listens
well he who carefully notes this".

Notwithstanding, I continued speaking to
Ser Brunetto, and I asked who were his
most distinguished and notable companions.

And he replied: "To know of a few is good;
of others it is better to be silent, as time
would be too short for the discourse needed.

Therefore, know that all were clerics and
great men of letters of inordinate fame,
whose lives were polluted by the same sin.

Priscian is with that despaired crowd, and
also Francesco d'Accorso; and you could've
seen if you really wanted to, that filthy one

that the servant of servants transferred
from the Arno to Bacchiglione, where
he abandoned his evilly inclined nerves.

I would tell you more; but this walk and
conversation cannot extend further, as I
see new smoke elevating from the sandpit.

People come with whom I must not mix.
I commend to you my Treasure, in which
the memory of me lives on, I ask no more".

He then turned, and seemed of those
that run on Verona's fields to win
the green cloth; and of these seems

the winner, not the one who loses.

Canto XVI

The poets continue in the circle of the violent and Dante hears the thunderous sound of water falling into the next level. He is immediately identified by three souls, once prominent, due to his Florentine accent and they sprint towards him calling out that he wait for them. The spokesperson Iacopo Rusticucci introduces Guido Guerra and Tegghiaio Aldobrandi, adding that he is in this circle on account of his vexatious wife. Dante is spurned by a desire to embrace them but the danger of raining fire prevents it. Instead, he honours them saying he knows of them by reputation and is filled with sorrow at their condition. They have heard disturbing things about Florence from Guiglielmo Borsiere who only recently joined them. Dante confirms their concerns and, admiring Dante's succinct reply, they sprint off in an instant. This again creates the impression of the supernatural speed previously seen in Canto XV when Ser Brunetto sprints back to his companions; and Canto XIII when Nessus leads the poets once more across the Phlegethon and they instantly find themselves in the forest. The poets continue and come closer to the deafening waterfall, when Virgil takes the cord from around Dante's waist and casts one end over the cliff's edge. The drama now leaves the pathos of human encounter as Dante forewarns of embarking on an encounter with a bizarre creature whose metaphorical significance is a complex amalgam.

Dante's Inferno

I arrived wherein the echo could be heard
of water descending into the next circle,
similar to the buzzing sound of beehives,

when three spirits took off together
from a group travelling and sprinted
under that rain of bitter torment.

Coming towards us, each was crying:
"Stop you whose clothes seem to
tell you are of our depraved city".

Oh my, what sores I saw on their members
from searing flames, both recent and old!
It still pains me only thinking about them.

On hearing, my Master heeded their cries:
turned his face to me, and "Now wait",
he said, "we must be courteous towards these.

Were it not for the natural fire fulminating
this place, I would say urgency to meet
be on your part rather than on theirs".

As we had stopped, they repeated the
same song and upon their reaching us,
all three drew together to form a wheel.

Similarly to naked and oiled wrestlers,
assessing another's grip and leverage,
before striking and lunging at each other,

thus they turned, each with his gaze
fixed on me, so their necks twisted
away from the direction of their steps.

Canto XVI

And one said: "If the misery of this unstable
sand and our burned, scorched off skin
causes us and our requests to be despised,

may our repute still compel your spirit
to say who you are, whose living feet
carry you confidently through this hell.

He whose footsteps you see me follow,
though he is going naked and flayed,
had such status you cannot imagine:

he was grandson to the gallant Gualdrada;
his name was Guido Guerra, and in his life
distinguished himself in intellect and valour.

The other who tramples the sand behind me,
is Tegghiaio Aldobrandi, whose voice should
have been more appreciated on earth above.

And I, who with them have been crucified,
was Iacopo Rusticucci, and certainly above
all else was harmed by my shrew of a wife".

If I could have been covered against the fire,
I would have thrown myself amongst them,
and think the doctor would have suffered it;

but as I would be burned and cooked,
fear conquered the strong desire
that had filled me to embrace them.

Then I began: "Not scorn, but sorrow
for your condition so fills me within,
it will take me a long time to dissipate,

as soon as this Master of mine uttered
words by which I imagined you to be,
so indeed you came and are as he said.

I am from your city, and always did
affectionately hear of and reference
your works and honoured names.

I leave behind bile for sweet fruit
as promised by my truthful guide;
but I must descend to the centre".

"Then long may your soul direct
the limbs you have", he replied,
"and your future fame resplend,

do tell if courtesy and valour still
reside in our city as was customary,
or if have entirely abandoned her;

as Guiglielmo Borsiere, who but recently
suffers with us and walks there with our
mates, disturbs us much with his words".

"Florence, new citizens and quick riches
have generated pride and excess in you,
so you already suffer the aftereffects".

Thus did I cry out with uplifted face;
the three, taking it as my response,
eyed each other as if struck by truth.

"If it costs you so little other times",
all replied, "to satisfy others' enquiries,
happy are you for such able speaking!

Canto XVI

So, if you survive these dark places
and return to again see beautiful stars,
when it befits you to say 'I was there',

make it so you tell people about us".
At which they broke up and ran off
their lithe legs as if flapping wings.

You could not have said an 'amen'
in the time they took to disappear;
and leaving seemed timely to Master.

I was following him, having just left,
and the sound of water was so close,
we were at pains to hear one another.

Like that river's entire course that runs
from Monte Viso towards the East,
along the left side of the Apennines,

called Acquacheta at the top, before
it descends into the lower bed,
and at Forli comes to lose the name,

roaring above San Benedetto dell'Alpe
to fall into the one waterfall, whereas
it could be received by one thousand;

so then, down from a plunging ravine,
we found the echoing of that red river,
that in no time would damage our ears.

I had a cord tied around my waist,
and had thought once to use it
to capture the leopard with painted hide.

After I had loosened it completely from
around me as my guide commanded,
I handed it over to him all rolled up.

At which he turned to his right flank,
threw it some length from the edge
with it falling into that deep abyss.

"Yet something new must respond",
I said to myself, "to Master's unusual sign
that he follows up with a keen eye".

Oh my, how careful men must be when
with those who do not just see actions,
whose intellect scrutinises thought itself!

He said to me: "But soon will rise here
what I await and your thoughts imagine;
which will reveal itself to your very eyes".

Man as much as possible must close his lips
in uttering truths that appear to be lies,
which though faultless mark him the liar;

but here I cannot be silent; and by the notes
of this Comedìa, oh reader, I swear, so may
they not be denied longstanding favour,

that I saw along that heavy dark air
come swimming upwards a figure,
striking to the most courageous of heart,

as returns he who descended to disentangle
an anchor entangled under a rock or
other object covered over by the sea,

extending arms and retracting legs below.

Canto XVII

The creature, Geryon, is introduced to the reader as an embodiment that crushes all opposition and pervades humanity. Its physical features reflect its deception[1], viciousness[2] and associated cruelty. Virgil, arguably in his role as metaphor for reason, negotiates the unpredictable creature's assistance to descend into the next circle. In the meantime, Dante visits the usurers suffering on the sand nearby, scalded by its burning and scorched by the descending flames, trying desperately to relieve the pain using their hands. He does not recognise them individually but notes the purses hung around their necks with the crests of the Gianfigliazzi, Ubriachi, and Scrovegni families. Anxious to get back to his guide, Dante hurries and finds Virgil already mounted on Geryon. With trepidation he joins Virgil who has placed himself between Dante and the stinging tail and who tightly embraces him. The creature begins its slow descent and Dante is given a terrifying macroscopic view of hell. Upon landing, Geryon, disgruntled, disposes of the travellers and once again Dante uses the image of accelerated movement as the creature disappears from sight at the speed of an arrow shot from a bow.

---

1   The beast's face is that of the just man: *La faccia sua era faccia d'uom giusto*. Its features are ornate and enticing: *lo dosso e 'l petto e ambedue le coste, dipinti avea di nodi e di rotelle.*
2   Its tail's sting is that of a scorpion flicking in the void, suggesting an unpredictable threat: *Nel vano tutta sua coda guizzava*. Its ferocity is seen in the fur on its limbs: *due branche avea pilose insin l'ascelle;*

Dante's Inferno

"See the beast with the pointed tail, traversing
mounts, smashing through walls and weapons!
See she whose stench does pollute the world!".

Thus my Master began speaking to me;
while motioning for it to come ashore
near to the end of our traversed marble.

And that filthy symbol of fraud
came, landing head and chest,
but not its tail, upon the edge.

Its face was that of a just man,
so benign was its countenance,
the remainder was serpentine;

two taloned limbs hairy to its armpits;
its back and chest and both sides were
embellished in artistic twists and curls.

Never more colour in backdrop and relief
were fabrics woven by Tartars or Turks,
nor Arachne such complex web warped.

As when barges sometimes moored,
partly in water and partly on shore,
as there among drunkard Germans

the beaver is poised to catch its prey,
so the foul beast stood at the rocky
edge that circumscribes the sand.

Its whole tail was flicking in the void,
twisting up its venomous fork whose
tip was armed as that of a scorpion.

Canto XVII

My Master said: "We must now deviate
somewhat from our path towards that
savage beast that is located over there".

So we descended to our right,
and took ten steps along the edge,
to keep the sand and flames at bay.

And when we had reached it,
a little further on I saw the damned
sitting on the sand at the cliff's edge.

My Master: "so that you may have
a complete experience of this ring",
told me "go, see the state they are in.

Your discourse there must be short;
till you return, I will speak to this one,
that it lend us its powerful shoulders".

So further up I went all on my own to
the outer extreme of the seventh circle
to where those dejected people sat.

Their sorrow exploded from their eyes;
with hands flicking away left and right
firstly at flames, then at scalding sands:

no differently behave dogs in summer
now with snout then with paw, bitten
either by fleas or flies or horseflies.

Having looked at some of the faces,
on which the dolorous fire descends,
I did not recognise any; but I realised

each had a purse around their necks with
particular colours and particular crests,
that their eye seemed nurtured by them.

And as I walked among them observing,
I saw a pouch with a blue lion's face
and poised form on yellow background.

Then, as my gaze continued to survey,
I saw another one that was blood red,
displaying a goose whiter than butter.

And one with pregnant blue sow
adorning his white pouch, said:
"what are you doing in this pit?

Go get lost, and as you are still living,
know that my fellow citizen Vitaliano
will soon be sitting here to my left.

I am Paduan here by these Florentines:
many times do they thunder deafening
me: "May the sovereign knight come,

bringing the pouch with three goats!".
Now distorting his mouth he poked out
his tongue, as does an ox licking its snout.

And I, fearing remaining would bother
he who warned to remain a short time,
turned back from those depleted souls.

I found my Master already mounted
on the back of the ferocious animal,
telling me: "Now be strong and brave.

Canto XVII

So now descent must be by such stairs;
mount in front, as I want to be between
you and the tail so it cannot hurt you".

As he so overcome with cold shivers
of Quartan fever, nails already livid,
shakes all over just seeing the shade,

so became I at said words; but shame
did make her threats, and strengthen
the servant before a valorous master.

I sat on the awful, gigantic shoulders;
wanting to say what I thought but lacked
the words: "make sure you do hug me".

But he, who had other times aided me
in uncertainty, as soon as I mounted
embraced and therefore sustained me;

and said: "now Geryon, off you go: be
sure you turn broadly in slow descent;
mindful of the unusual weight you carry".

As a small boat leaves where berthed,
reversing bit by bit, so too it detached;
and when it felt completely underway,

it turned its tail towards where its chest
had been and extended it, sharp as an eel,
with its legs gathering the air unto itself.

I do not think there was any more fear
in Phaëthon when he released the reigns,
whereby the sky, as seen today, burned;

Dante's Inferno

Nor when miserable Icarus felt feathers
plucked from his back's melted wax,
as his father shouted "Wrong way!",

as was mine, when I saw nothing
but air all round me, and all else
disappeared other than the beast.

So it swam slowly slowly; turning and
descending, without my realising it but
by the wind in my face and underneath.

I could now hear the maelstrom to my right
creating a terrible roar underneath us,
at which I stuck out my head to gaze below.

Then I felt more fear of plummeting,
as I saw fires and heard the wailing;
thus trembling, I squeezed my thighs.

And then I saw, what I'd not seen before,
descending and turning to great horrors
now encroaching upon us from all sides.

As a falcon long riding steady air,
without having sighted lure or prey causes
the Falconer to say "oh, you descend!",

descends fatigued, by a hundred circles
to where had taken off, and lands distant
from his master, indignant and vexatious;

so Geryon put us down at the bottom,
at the very foot of the ragged rockface,
and, having shrugged off our persons,

disappeared as if shot from a bow.

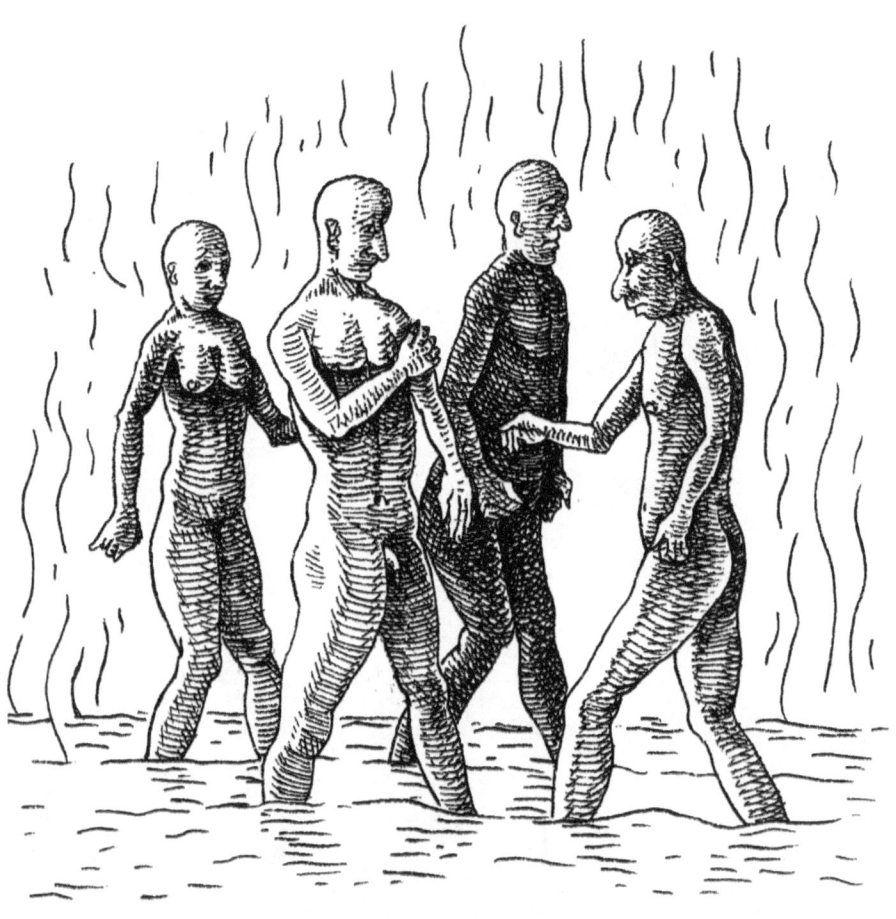

Canto XVIII

Dante's aerial descent into the eighth circle called *Malebolge* (evil pits) permits him to describe the ten concentric *bolge* contained within it with their footbridges linking them. In the first *bolgia* are two single files of naked sinners, each file going in a direction opposite to the other. One has pimps, the other seducers. Dante recognises Venedico Caccianemico who reluctantly admits to having prostituted his own sister, Ghisolabella to the lust of the Marquis. Virgil indicates the still regal Jason on the other hand for his seduction of Hypsipyle. As they approach the second bank, the travellers encounter a terrible stench and soon discover that the damned are the flatterers wading in excrement. Dante converses with Alessio Interminei who despairs of his penchant for flattery. Virgil then points out Thais the harlot also guilty of that sin.

Dante's Inferno

Hell has a place called Malebolge,
made out of iron coloured stone,
like the rock walls that enclose it.

Right in the middle of the maleficent plain
opens a pit that is very wide and deep,
of whose structure I will tell in due course.

The residual space forms a circular belt
between the pit and the high rock wall,
and its base is segmented into ten bolge.

For which as protection of the walls
multiple moats encircle the castles;
the layout having deliberate design,

such was the image they created here;
and as fortresses have their footbridges
from the thresholds to furthest banks,

so from the base of the rockface extended
stone bridges intersecting banks and ditches
to the pit that terminates and collects them.

In this place, we found ourselves thrust
off from Geryon's back; and the poet
took to the left, and I followed him.

To our right I saw the new anguish,
new torture and new flagellators,
of which this first bolgia was replete.

At the base of the pit were naked sinners;
in the half closest they walked facing us,
the rest walked along with us, but faster,

Canto XVIII

as the Romans directed the multitudes,
in the year of the Jubilee, having found
the way for people to cross the bridge,

that on one side all were heading
to the castle and then St. Peter's,
and on the other side to the mount.

Over here and over there on black rock
I saw horned demons with large whips,
who cruelly lashed them on their backs.

Oh how they made them take to their
heels with the first lashes! None at all
awaited their second or third stroke.

As I went my way, mine eyes met those
of one of them; and I quickly said: "This
is not the first time I've set eyes on him".

So I stopped to better scrutinise him;
and my kind guide stopped with me,
and assented for me to go back a bit.

And that flagellated one thought to hide
lowering his face; but it did little good,
as I said: "hey you with downcast eyes,

if the features you bear do not lie, you
are Venedico Caccianemico. What brings
you here to swallow such a bitter pill?".

And he replied: "I answer reluctantly;
but am compelled by your precise words,
that take me back to a world since passed.

I am the one who led Ghisolabella
to satisfy the whims of the marquis,
whichever way the sordid story be told.

And am not the only Bolognese crying here;
indeed this place is so full of them,
that not this many tongues have learned

to say 'yes' between Sàvena and Reno;
and if you need a pledge or testimony,
draw to mind our proclivity for greed".

As he was speaking a demon struck him
with leather whip saying: "away with you,
pimp! There are no women to con here".

I met up again with my guide; and
after a few steps we were where the
ridge protruded from the bank.

We climbed onto it effortlessly;
turning right on the craggy surface,
so departing from that eternal circling.

When we arrived where it rises leaving
a path below for the scourged to travel,
the guide said: "Wait, allow these other

illegitimate souls to set their eyes on you,
whose faces you haven't seen yet as they
were going in the same direction as us".

From the ancient bridge we saw the line
that came to us from the other side,
similarly driven along by the lashings.

Canto XVIII

And the good Master, without my asking,
said: "Look at that imposing one coming,
crying but not shedding tears of pain:

what regal demeanour he still retains!
He is Jason, whose courage and sagacity
deprived the Colchians of the golden fleece.

He travelled to the island of Lemnos
after the cruel and ruthless women
had previously killed all of the men.

There using enticing words and gestures
he fooled Hypsipyle, that young woman
who earlier deceived all the other women.

He abandoned her there pregnant, alone;
this sin condemns him to this punishment;
and for Medea also is revenge taken.

With him go whoever deceives this way;
and enough said about the first valley
and those souls whom it mauls within".

We soon arrived where the narrow path
intersects with the second bank, at which
it acts as support for another arch.

There we heard people lamenting
and snorting in the other bolgia,
striking themselves with their palms.

The banks were encrusted with a mould
from the fumes below and of it pasted,
offensive to the eye and sense of smell.

The base was so cavernous that nowhere
allows seeing into it than climbing atop
the arch, where the bridge is at its highest.

There we arrived; and down below
I saw people tossed in an excrement
seemingly come of human latrines.

And while scouring the pit's base,
I saw one with head so covered in filth,
you could not say if he was lay or cleric.

He yelled disapprovingly: "why so anxious
to watch me more than the other filth?".
And I: "Because, if I remember correctly,

I have already seen you with dry hair
and you are Alessio Interminei of Lucca:
hence I eye you more than all the others".

And he then, bashing his head said:
"Flattery, that my tongue never grew
tired of has submerged me down here ".

After which my guide said "Make the
effort, push your gaze a bit further on,
so your eye captures clearly the face

of that filthy whore with unkempt hair
scratching herself with faeces-filled nails,
now crouching, now standing up straight.

She is Thais, the harlot who when asked
by her lover 'do you see me having great
merit?' replied 'not great, extraordinary!'.

We have seen enough of all this".

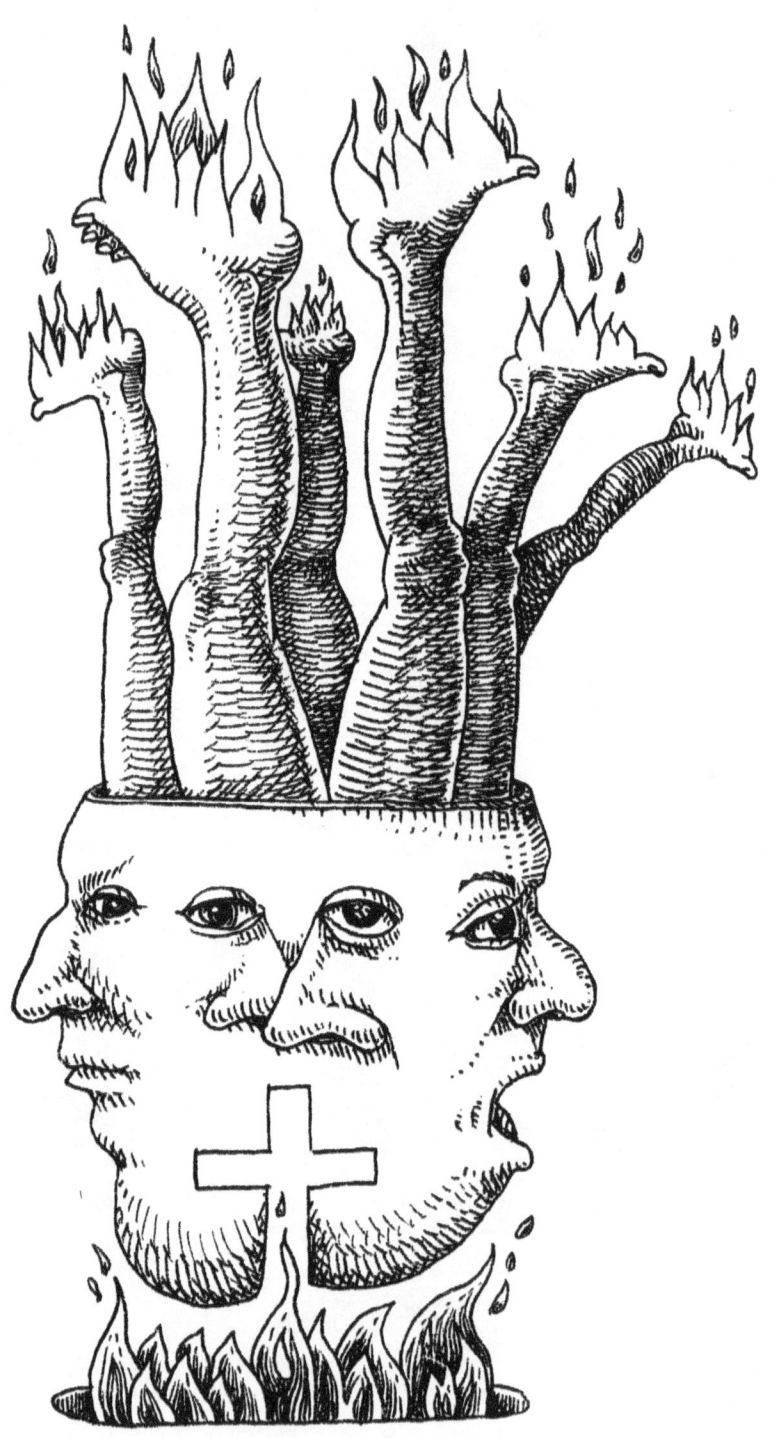

Canto XIX

Dante the poet begins this Canto at the third bolgia railing against the ones who practice simony, those who derive personal gain from holy office. These are inserted head first into holes in the rock with legs protruding and feet aflame. As an aside, Dante compares the holes to the baptismal fonts at San Giovanni, one of which he declares he once broke while saving someone from drowning. He proceeds to unreservedly condemn popes Nicholas III, Boniface VIII and Clement V who are destined to succeed each other with each of the second two driving the former further into their assigned hole. After addressing Nicholas III's mistaking him for Boniface VIII having arrived prematurely, Dante launches a diatribe against Nicholas III and other shepherds who abused their positions of power. This pleases Virgil, who takes Dante up and delivers him to the next bolgia.

Oh Simon Magus, oh miserable disciples,
that God's matters rather than being
betrothed to goodness, by rapaciousness

for gold and silver, you adulterate;
now must the trumpet sound for you,
because you are in the third bolgia.

We were already at the subsequent tomb,
positioned on the bridge at the point
perpendicular to the centre of the pit.

Oh sublime wisdom, what great art you
show in Heaven, earth and the bad world,
and what justice does your virtue bestow!

I saw along the rockface and pit's base
the bruised coloured rock full of holes,
all of the same size and each was round.

They didn't seem narrower or wider
than at my beautiful San Giovanni,
built as a place to conduct baptisms;

one of which, not too many years ago
I broke to save one from drowning in:
may this seal the truth, undeceiving all.

From each hole's mouth there issued
feet and legs of a sinner to his thighs,
whilst the remainder stayed inside.

All had the soles of their feet aflame;
so that they shook their joints so hard
they could snap wicker and grass rope.

Canto XIX

As flames on unctuous substances
move only along the outer surface,
so it was from the heels to their toes.

"Who is that, Master, more furiously
spasming than do his companions",
said I, "that a redder flame sucks?".

And he said: "if you wish me to take
you down along the lower bank,
he will tell who he is and of his sin".

And I: "What pleases you, pleases me:
you as guide know well I won't ignore
your will, you know hidden thoughts".

Then we came to the fourth embankment;
we turned and descended left
down to the narrow bottom full of holes.

My good Master still held me to his hip
until he had taken me to the hole of the
one who was lamenting with his shanks.

"Oh whoever you are there upside down,
tragic soul as stake driven in the ground",
I began to say, "speak if you are able".

I was like a friar hearing the confession
of a perfidious killer, who, once positioned,
calls out to him so as to delay the execution.

He cried: "Are you already here on your feet,
Are you here standing erect, Boniface?
The text has cheated me of several years.

Are you already satisfied with the wealth
for which you did not fear deceiving the
lovely woman, and then devastating her?".

I became like those left confused,
not understanding the reply given,
as if scoffed at, and cannot respond.

Then Virgil said: "Tell him quickly: 'I am
not he, I am not the one you think I am'";
and I replied as I was instructed to.

At which the soul's feet all contorted;
then sighing and with a tearful voice,
said: "Well what is it that you want?

If knowing who I am so compels you,
that you have come down the bank,
know that I wore the great mantle;

and as legitimate son of the she-bear,
was greedy to advance my cubs, and to
fill my pockets, so I now fill a pocket.

Under my head are others drawn
preceding me in practising simony,
squashed into fissures in the rock.

I too will fall further with the advent
of he whom I thought that you were,
when hastily asking that question.

But greater is my time with feet cooked
and having been upside down like this
than he to be thus planted with fiery feet:

Canto XIX

after him comes one of worse deeds,
from the west, an outlaw shepherd
suited to covering both him and me.

He will be the new Jason we read of in
Maccabees: as to him the king softened,
so too will behave this French sovereign".

I am not sure if I was too brazen,
when I answered him in this tone:
"So, tell me: how much treasure

did Our Lord want from St Peter before
entrusting the keys to him? Certainly
he requested no more than 'Follow me'.

Neither Peter nor others took Matthew's
gold or silver, when they cast lots
to fill that guilty soul's place.

So stay here, as is your just punishment;
and keep the money obtained in deceit
that made you so opposed to Charles.

And if it were not for my veneration
of the sublime keys you held when
in the happy life that holds me back,

I would use far more severe words;
as your avarice saddens the world,
treading on the good, lifting the wicked.

You shepherds were noted by the
Evangelist, when seeing she who sits
on the waters copulating with kings;

she who was born with the seven heads,
that drew strength from the ten horns,
as long as her husband did love virtue.

You made a god of gold and silver; what
distinguishes you from the idolater, but
that he one adores, and you a hundred?

Oh, Constantine, what evil mothered,
not your conversion, but your dowry
received by the first wealthy Father!".

And while clearly singing this, whether
from biting anger or burning conscience,
he was kicking wildly with both legs.

I strongly believe this pleased my guide,
who with a smiling face hung on every
manifestly true word that left my lips.

So he wrapped me in his arms;
and after lifting me to his chest,
mounted the path he had descended.

Nor did he tire of embracing me,
taking me to the peak of the arch
linking the fourth and fifth banks.

There he gently put down his load,
delicately on steep and rough rock
a place of hard work even for goats.

There another valley was revealed to me.

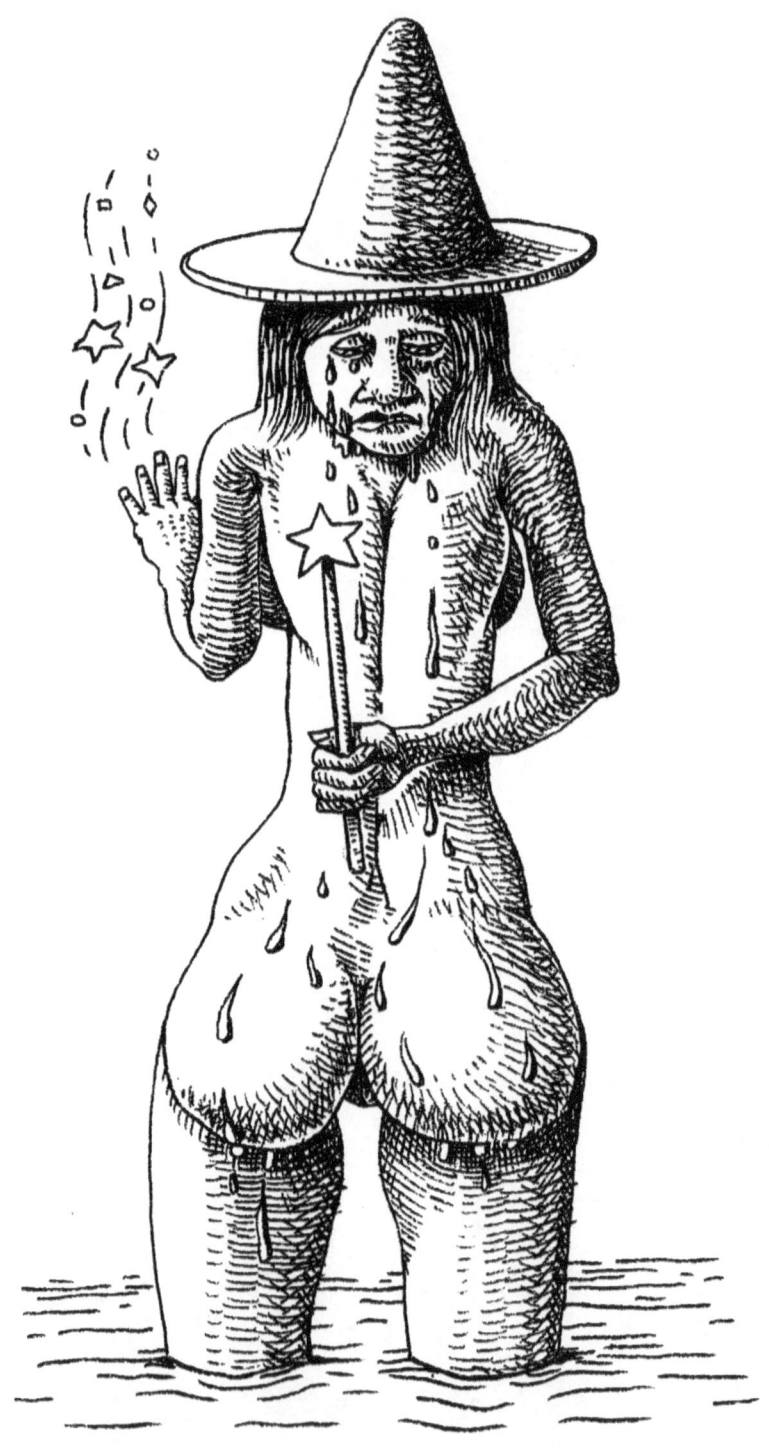

Canto XX

Dante unusually expresses self-consciousness at the beginning of this Canto as to exercising his craft. He then proceeds to describe the souls contained in this bolgia who must walk backwards on account of their heads being twisted around 180 degrees. These are the sorcerers and diviners who in life usurped God, predicting people's future in contradiction to the ordained use of personal Faith in God's purpose. Their condemnation, as they weep with tears falling to their buttocks is to never see what is ahead of them again, eternally. Dante is himself driven to tears out of sympathy and is roundly reprimanded by Virgil. Here Dante the pilgrim, with his continuing human failings, is instructed that once in hell a soul should not be afforded any altruistic consideration. Virgil then points out Amphiaraus, Tiresias, Aruns and finally Manto who founded Mantua on hitherto uninhabited land, grounding it in her dark arts. Others of note that he identifies are Eurypylus, Michael Scot, Guido Bonatti and Asdente.

Dante's Inferno

I must create verses of new agony
as material for the twentieth Canto
of the first song, of the submerged.

I was already well prepared to look
into the visible base of the chasm,
that was soaked in tears of anguish;

and I saw people within the round pit
come, silent and crying, at the gait
of litanies in processions on earth.

As soon as I looked further down at them,
amazingly it seemed each was twisted
at the neck, between the chin and chest

so the faces were turned towards the rear,
and they were made to walk backwards,
having been denied their view forwards.

Perhaps a paralytic may have already
been contorted this way; but I have
never seen it, nor believe it happens.

Reader, may God allow you to harvest
from your reading, now think yourself
how I could manage to keep a dry eye,

when so near to me I saw human form
so distorted, the tears from their eyes
wetting the crack of their buttocks.

I promptly wept, propped on a protrusion
of the rocky bridge, so that my guide said:
"so are you too like all these other fools?

Canto XX

Here true pity is indeed to have none;
who is the more wicked than the one
who imposes his will on divine justice?

Raise your head, lift it, and see he under
whom earth opened before the Thebans,
as all shouted: 'Where are you falling to,

Amphiaraus? Why do you leave the war?'.
His precipitation in the abyss didn't stop
till reaching Minos who seizes them all.

See his shoulders converted into his chest;
due to his pretence of seeing so far ahead,
he looks back while he walks backward.

See there Tiresias, who morphed form
when of a man a woman he became,
as all his body's members he altered;

and before regaining his male crest
he had to take his rod and again hit
the two intertwining serpents.

Aruns is whose back is at this one's belly
who in the mountains of Luni, where toil
the Carraresi who inhabit the plain below,

had a cave amongst the white marble
as a home; from which could see stars
and sea with an unobstructed view.

And that one with covered breasts
that you cannot see, and loose locks,
with pubic hair to the other side, was

Manto, who wandered over many lands;
finally settling there where I was born;
of which I ask you to listen a moment.

After her father had passed from this life
and the city of Bacchus became enslaved,
she wandered a long time in the world.

On earth in beautiful Italy extends a lake,
at the foot of the Alps bordering Germany
near the Tyrol, that has the name Benaco.

A thousand rills and more, I think, bathe
Alpine areas from Garda to Val Camonica,
with water that comes to stagnate in the lake.

At its centre is where the shepherd
of Trent, and Brescia and of Verona
could bless if perchance went there.

There is Peschiera, fortress solid and lovely,
able to confront Brescians and Bergamese,
placed where the shoreline is at its lowest.

Here perforce all the water tipping
the bosom of Benaco spills and
becomes a river in green fields below.

As soon as this water begins to flow,
no longer is it Benaco, but Mencio
till Governol, where it flows to the Po.

After a short run, it finds a depression,
where it extends forming swamp land;
and scarcity in summer can make it putrid.

Canto XX

The savage virgin, passing by there
saw land in the swamp's centre,
uncultivated and bereft of any dweller.

Settling to avoid all human interaction,
devoting herself and ghosts to her arts;
so lived, and there left her void cadaver.

Later, the neighbourhood inhabitants
assembled in the place, defended
by the bog around it in every direction.

They founded the city on her dead bones
honouring she who first chose the place,
unreliant on spells, they named it Mantua.

Once, numerous people lived there,
prior to Casalodi's foolishness being
taken advantage of by Pinamonte.

So I counsel you that, if you ever hear
that my land has had diverse origins,
no lie is able to deny the very truth".

And I: "Master, your statements are so
strong and gain my trust to such extent,
other assertions are mere embers spent.

But do tell, of those that are passing,
whether you see anyone noteworthy;
as my mind only focusses on this now".

Then he said: "He whose beard falls from
his cheeks onto those darkened shoulders,
was – when Greece was devoid of men,

so rare as only found in cradles – an augur,
who with Calchas, portended the propitious
time to cut the first mooring ropes at Aulis.

Eurypylus was his name, so named in
a particular passage in my great poem:
as by knowing it all, you well know.

That other one with such thin loins,
was Michael Scot, who knew only too
well the deceptive art of magic tricks.

See there Guido Bonatti; see Asdente who
now wishes he had dedicated himself
to leather and laces, but repents too late.

See the wicked women who left the needle,
spool and spindle, becoming fortune tellers;
casting incantations with herbs and images.

Now let's go, as Cain with thorns touches
the limits of both hemispheres and
is setting below the sea near Seville;

indeed last night under a full moon:
you remember as it was not a bad
thing at times in the deep forest".

So he spoke, and meanwhile we walked.

Canto XXI

The travellers continue to converse as they reach the peak of the next bridge and Dante notes the unremitting lament of those in the utter darkness. At the base of the pit, he describes an infernal, bubbling pitch comparing it to the pitch used to repair ships' hulls in the maritime State of Venice. Unexpectedly, with Dante frightened by Virgil's alert, a vicious demon strides along the bridge with a clawed soul thrown over his shoulder and tosses it into the pitch. Its torment begins immediately and the demon announces there are more corrupt Chief Magistrates to come from Santa Zita (the patron Saint of Lucca). Virgil then instructs Dante to hide behind a rock while he approaches the congregation of demons. These instinctively begin to attack, yet Virgil warns that they elect one of them to listen before deciding whether to hook him. Malacoda is chosen and approaches Virgil who asks whether he has considered how the two travellers could have survived their journey to that point but for Divine Will and Providence. At these words the demon's resolve is crushed and he instructs the others not to harm them. Virgil calls Dante out and the Malebranche demons move aggressively towards him. Scarmiglione entertains hooking Dante but is immediately reprimanded by Malacoda. The latter explains that the next bridge collapsed five hours short of 1,266 years previously (meaning the Harrowing of Hell between the death and resurrection of Jesus). Therefore, he would provide an escort to take them to another bridge that would allow them to proceed on their journey. The escort consists of demons some of whose names translate their bestiality more easily than others: Alichino, Calcabrina, Cagnazzo, Barbariccia, Libicocco, Draghignazzo,

Ciriatto, Graffiacane, Farfarello, and Rubicante. Their departure includes a salutation particular to their vulgarity: the ten salute Malacoda with their tongues pressed against their teeth; while the leader of the ten responds by breaking wind in their direction.

Canto XXI

So bridge to bridge, we conversed widely
beyond what my Comedìa sings of, and
came and stood at the arch's peak, when

we stopped to observe the next opening
of Malebolge and the other pointless crying;
and I saw that it was extraordinarily dark.

As seen in the Venetian Arsenal in
winter where boils the dense pitch
to recoat their damaged ships,

as are unable to be sailed – instead
some restore vessels and others plug
the sides of those that have sailed much;

some hammer bow and some stern;
others make oars and others fold ropes;
some repair mainsail and mizzen:

so too, not by fire but divine arts,
did a thick pitch boil down there,
smearing the banks on both sides.

I could see the pitch, but nothing within
apart from the bubbles that bubbled up,
all of it inflating, then collapsing.

While I was looking down intently,
my guide called "Look out, Look out!",
pulling me to him from where I stood.

I then turned as he who anxious to
see that from which should escape,
and fear makes suddenly impotent,

while looking still does not slow
his fleeing: as I saw behind us a black
demon running up along that bridge.

My, how ferocious he was in appearance
and how cruel he seemed in demeanour,
with open wings and so fleet footed!

His shoulder was held high and sharp,
bearing on it a sinner by the rump,
claws holding him tightly at the ankles.

From our bridge he yelled: "Malebranche,
here is one of Santa Zita's elders!
Shove him in, as I shall return again to

that city, as it is well furnished with these:
everyman is a conman, except Bonturo;
money turning every 'no' into a 'yes'".

He thrust him down, and on the rocky bridge
turned round, and never was there a mastiff
unleashed as hurriedly in pursuit of a thief.

The soul dived, resurfacing prayerfully
posed; but the devils beneath the bridge
cried: "The Holy Face isn't venerated here!

here we swim differently to the Serchio!
So, if you want to avoid our gaffing,
do not resurface from the pitch".

Then piercing with more than hundred hooks,
shrieked: "here you dance covered over,
so, if able, you can seize under cover".

Canto XXI

No differently do cooks get kitchen hands
to plunge meat in the middle of the pot
using their prongs, so that it cannot float.

The Master said: "So it is not evident
you are here, crouch behind a rocky
outcrop, that offers you some cover;

as for any offence committed against me,
do not be afraid, as I have it under control,
having had this kind of squabbling before".

He then crossed to the bridge's other end;
and reaching the edge of the sixth bank, it
served him to have an air of conviction.

With the same furore and clamour dogs
have when setting upon a poor mendicant
who begs where stopped in his tracks,

so these came out from under the bridge,
and aimed all their hooks towards him;
but he cried: "Let none show evil intent!

Before you use your prongs to hook me,
let one of you come forward to listen,
and then take counsel if I am to be gaffed".

All screamed out: "Malacoda must go!";
so the one moved – others staying firm –
he went saying: "how can this help him?".

"Have you considered, Malacoda, seeing
I come here", said my Master, "already
protected from all your impediments, it

is not due to divine will and providence?
Leave us be, that in Heaven it is willed
that I show another this savage walk".

At this, his arrogance was so crushed,
that his hook fell to his feet, telling
the others: "So be it, don't wound him".

And my Master to me: "Oh you there
squatting among the bridge's rocks,
confidently you can now return to me".

I then stood and sped towards him;
and the devils all surged forward so
I feared would not maintain the pact.

So too had I already seen soldiers fearfully
exit the Caprona castle under the truce,
landing amongst so many of their foes.

I grabbed my guide with my entire
person, and did not take my eyes off
their demeanour which was not good.

They stood hooks poised telling each
other "shall I tap him on the buttock?".
And all replied: "Yes, let him have it".

But that demon who was conversing with
my Master spun around immediately and
said: "Stand down, settle, Scarmiglione!".

He then said: "Continuing on this series
of stoney bridges isn't possible, because
the sixth one lies demolished in the pit.

Canto XXI

And if proceeding is still what you intend,
do both continue up this embankment;
nearby is another ridge that gives access.

Yesterday, five hours from present time,
one thousand two hundred and sixty six
years passed since the bridge crumbled.

I will send these of mine along to see if
anyone is out and about from the pitch:
go with them, they will not hurt you".

"Front and centre, Alichino, and Calcabrina",
he began, "and you too Cagnazzo;
and Barbariccia can lead the ten.

Libicocco will join you, Draghignazzo too,
Ciriatto with his tusks and Graffiacane
and Farfarello and the rabid Rubicante.

Scour all around the boiling pitch;
they must safely reach the other bridge
that traverses all the dens at once".

"Oh dear me, Master, what is this I see?",
I said, "if you know the way, let's go alone,
without escort, as I do not feel the need.

If you are as attentive as usual, can you
not see them grinding their teeth
with eyes that threaten torment?".

And he to me: "I do not want you to fear;
let them grind as much as they wish,
as they do so for the boiling damned".

They turned onto the left bank; but
first each poked his tongue through
his teeth, as a salute to their leader;

and he made his bum into a trumpet.

Canto XXII

Dante derides the military communication of the escorting troop of ten by comparing them farcically to human military formality. Indeed, the blowing of raspberries and anal trumpeting of the demons at the end of Canto XXI is contrasted, tongue in cheek, in uniqueness with bagpipes. This continues as Dante describes the escort in a comical adaptation of Psalm 18:26: *with the pure you show yourself pure; and with the crooked you show yourself perverse.* His attention then focuses on those submerged and how they play cat and mouse with the demon Barbariccia by surfacing to relieve the agony and diving when potentially discovered. One soul fails to dive in time and is hooked and drawn out to be tortured. Dante steps forward to question him, who then declares his corruption when in service of the king. Meanwhile, Ciriatto uses one of his tusks to slice his body. Barbariccia steps in and protects the soul to enable the discussion to continue. The soul proceeds to respond to Virgil and speaks of another Italian in the pitch and offers to bring more of them to the demons. As a self serving negotiator he persuades the demons to hide while he attracts more souls. In contrast to the other demons, Alichino agrees and they all withdraw. The clever soul seizes the opportunity and dives into the pitch to free himself. The demons respond in pursuit but fail to reach him at which point two turn on each other in a clawing frenzy and fall into the pitch, requiring rescue from the others.

Dante's Inferno

I've previously seen cavalry break camp,
and start storming and go on parade,
and occasionally execute a retreat;

I have seen horsemen scouting your land,
oh Aretines, and seen incursions, fighting
in tournaments and competing in jousts;

at times to trumpets, other times to bells,
drums and visual signalling from castles,
and means both our own and foreign;

but never to such strange bagpipes have
I witnessed move horsemen or infantry,
nor ship sail to such sign from earth or star.

We were walking along with the ten devils.
O ferocious company! But in church keep
company with saints; in a bar, with drunks.

My eyes were firmly fixed on the pitch,
to observe all aspects within this bolgia
and of people inside it that were alight.

As when dolphins arch their backs
signalling seamen that they must
take measures to save their ships,

so at times, to lighten the suffering,
a sinner would expose his back and
hide it again as quick as a flash.

And as frogs at the surface of a ditch
hold their mouths out of the water,
hiding legs and the rest of the body,

Canto XXII

so too were the sinners in every direction;
but no sooner would Barbariccia approach,
they would submerge in the boiling pitch.

I saw, and still possess heartfelt horror,
when one, hesitated, as does occur
when a frog remains and another dives;

and Graffiacan, who was closest to him,
hooked into his pitch smeared locks and
drew him up, so he looked to me an otter.

I already knew the names of all of them,
noting them when they were picked out,
also when they called out to each other.

"Oh Rubicante be sure to sink your
claws into him, so that you flay him!",
shouted all the cursed ones in unison.

And I: "Master, if you are able to,
do find out who that vile one is now
fallen into the hands of his enemies".

My Master accosted him from one side; asking
what were his origins, and the other replied:
"I was born in the kingdom of Navarre.

My mother put me in the service
of a Lord, having had me with a villain,
destroyer of himself and of his things.

Then I entered the service of good King
Thibaut; there I took to being a bribe taker,
for which I do now compense in this heat".

And Ciriatto, from whose mouth issued
a tusk like that of a wild pig on each side,
gave him a taste of how one could slit.

The mouse had fallen amongst feral cats;
but Barbariccia shielded him with his arms
and said: "Stand back while I clutch him".

And he turned his face to my Master;
"Ask", he said, "if you wish to know more
from him, before the others shred him".

So my guide said: "Do tell: do you know
any of the other sinners under the pitch
who are Italians?". He replied: "I just left,

one who was a neighbour of that place.
If only I was still with him covered over,
so I would fear neither claw nor hook!".

And Libicocco said: "That's long enough,
and pierced his arm with the hook, so
that ripping it he took out a chunk of his arm.

Draghignazzo too sought to hook him
down at the legs; when the Decurion spun
round with a frowning look in the eye.

After they had all settled down a little,
while he was still looking at his wound,
my guide without hesitation asked him:

"Who was it you said you unfortunately
left behind in order to come to the shore?".
He replied: "It was Friar Gomita,

from Gallura, vessel of every fraud,
with firm hold of his Lord's enemies,
treating them such, each praised it.

Taking money for summary disposal of disputes,
as he puts it; also in his other offices he was
not a minor cheat, but sovereign over all.

Along with him is Don Michel Zanche
of Logodoro; and their tongues
are tirelessly wagging about Sardinia.

Oh my, look at the other baring his
teeth; I would say more, but I fear he
sets to give my ringworm a scratching".

The leader, turned to devilish Farfarello
who now glaring, threatened to strike,
saying: "Stand you back brazen bird!".

"If you want to see or hear", began
again the terrified one, "Tuscans or
Lombards, I will get some to come;

but let the Malebranche stand back,
so they do not fear their vengefulness;
and I, seated in this very spot, though on

my own, will make seven spirits come
when I whistle, as it is our thing to do
when one of us rears up from the pitch".

On hearing this Cagnazzo lifted his snout,
shaking his head, saying: "Hear the craftiness
he has excogitated so he can dive down!".

Dante's Inferno

Then he, whose snares were so abundant,
answered: "I am overly astute, particularly
if procuring greater suffering for friends".

Alichin could not contain himself and in
contrast to the others, said: if you dive,
I will not merely gallop after you,

rather I will flap my wings across the pitch.
Let's leave the ridge for the bank's shield,
and see if he can outdo all of us together".

So reader, you will now hear of a new contest:
each then turned their faces the other way,
the first being he most resistant to the plan.

The Navarrese picked the right moment;
pressing feet upon the rock, he instantly
leapt and freed himself from their intent.

At which each was stung by their guilt,
in particular he that caused the failure;
so he launched shouting: "You're caught!".

But it was of no use: as the wings could
not overtake fear itself; he going under,
while the other soared with lifted chest:

no differently does the duck instantly
dive when the falcon gets close, as the
latter flies high there angry and beaten.

Calcabrina, put out by the deception,
pursued him through the air, happy for
the escape so that he could have it out;

Canto XXII

and as soon as the swindler disappeared,
he turned his talons on his companion,
their claws gripping right above the pit.

But the other was a ready sparrowhawk
very capable with his talons, and both
fell into the middle of the boiling pond.

The heat quickly broke them up;
but taking flight was not possible,
so impregnated were their wings.

Barbariccia, despondent with his cohort,
ordered four to fly to the other side with
all their hooks, and they very rapidly

from here descended to their posts there;
extending hooks to they who were stuck,
already cooked within the pitch's crust.

And we left them thus in their quandary.

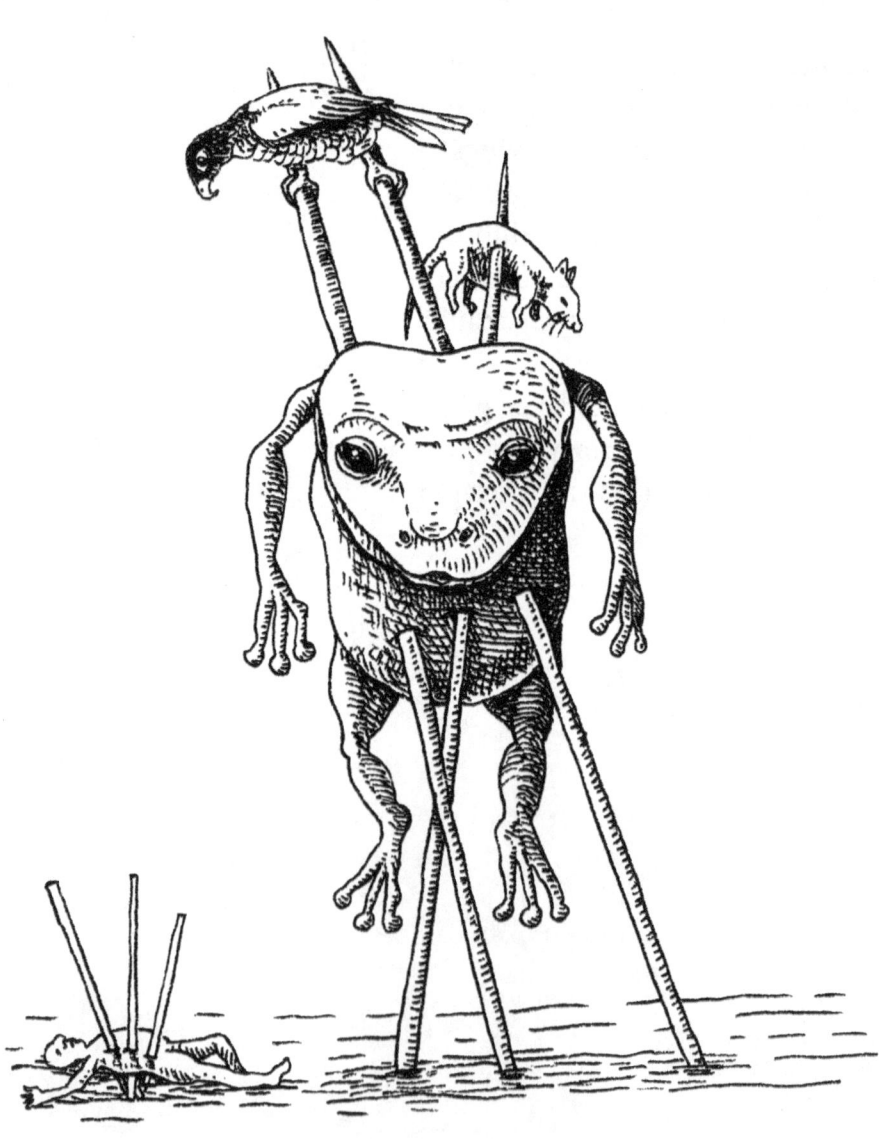

Canto XXIII

Dante the pilgrim reflects metaphorically on the complex human scenario of interdependency, betrayal and intervention by an observer. It is the case of the fable of the frog and mouse when the mouse requests assistance from the frog to cross the river. At the midway mark the frog decides to drown the mouse. However, a kite flying overhead sees the plight of the mouse and swoops down capturing and then killing both. Similarly, the Malbranche in their feigned benevolence in escorting the travellers in their care have lied about the destruction of the next bridge and the need for the escort. The consequences are potentially dire for the pilgrim and guide who come to realise their predicament and escape to the next level just as the demons with outstretched wings reveal their true intent. Having slid down the rocky slope, Dante and Virgil arrive safely at the sixth bolgia. Here they find the hypocrites weighed down by their sin symbolised by coats covered in gold but which are internally lined with lead. Their progress is retarded to a fraction of that of the travellers. The pilgrim's Tuscan pronunciation draws the attention of two souls who hurry as best they can to speak to him. They are Catalano dei Malavolti and Loderingo degli Andalò, friars of the Order of the glorious Saint Mary, otherwise known as the Jovial Friars. Dante begins talking to them when he is interrupted by the realisation of the High Priest Caiaphas skewered into the ground nearby with three stakes. This is his punishment for advising the Jewish leaders that it would be better for one man to die than the entire nation destroyed. His father-in-law Annas suffers a similar fate elsewhere. The travellers take direction from the friars and head to climb up the rockslide. Here Virgil angrily discovers that the bridge had collapsed here and that he had been lied to about the previous bridge collapse.

Dante's Inferno

Silently, alone, unaccompanied
we went, one ahead one behind,
as Franciscans do along the road.

My mind had turned to Aesop's fable
having witnessed the present conflict,
which tells of the frog and the mouse;

for the equivalence of 'now' and 'present'
is no closer than the fable to this fight, if
we attentively align beginnings to endings.

And as one thought springs from another,
so too was one born from the one prior,
then causing my original fear to double.

My thoughts were: "Due to us these
have been deceived and mocked, so
I think they are extremely irritated.

If anger compounds with ill will,
they will pursue us more viciously
than a dog readying to maul a hare".

I could now feel my hair stand on end
from the fear whilst looking over my
shoulder, I said: "Master, if you do not

hide yourself and me, as I do dread
the Malebranche. They're already behind
us; I imagine them such I already feel them.

And he: "Even if I were of leaded glass,
I could not reflect your external image
faster than capturing your internal sense.

Canto XXIII

Just now your thoughts mixed with mine,
with like inclination and with like form,
so that of both I made the one resolution.

If it is true the slope to the right inclines
permitting our descent to the next bolgia,
then we can avoid the envisioned attack.

He hadn't finished explaining the decision,
when I saw them not too distant coming
with outstretched wings, ready to take us.

My guide immediately grabbed me,
as the mother awakens to the noise
and sees the flames flaring near her,

not hesitating, seizes her child and flees
without even donning a shift; worrying
more for his welfare than for her own;

so from the summit of the hard bank
he launched supine on the rocky incline,
that seals one of the sides of the bolgia.

Water never did run in a canal as rapidly
when approaching the paddles so closely,
to turn the wheel of a mill on dry ground,

than Master on the edge of that shore,
taking me with him upon his chest,
as if I were his child, not a companion.

As soon as his feet reached the base of
the ditch, they arrived at the hill right
over us; but there was no need to fear:

for when divine providence wanted to
appoint them ministers of the fifth pit,
it took away the power of all to leave it.

Down there we found a painted people
that moved around with very slow gait,
crying and looking fatigued and crushed.

They wore mantles with hoods lowered
over their eyes, of a style in the manner
of that used for the monks in Cluny.

Externally they are golden so are blinding;
but internally they are all lead, so heavy
that those of Frederick were light as hay.

What a heavy mantle there for eternity!
We turned again now to our left in the
direction of those intent on sad crying;

but due to the weight the tired souls
went so slowly, that we were in new
company at each step that we took.

So I said to my guide: "Make it that you
find one recognisable by deed or name,
running your eye over them as we walk".

And one, hearing the Tuscan inflection,
from behind us yelled: "Slow down, you
walking hurriedly through the dismal air!

You may get from me what you are asking".
At which the guide turned and said: "Wait,
and then proceed according to his pace".

Canto XXIII

I halted and saw two, demonstrating great
anxiety on their faces, wanting to be with me;
but the weight and tight path slowed them.

Upon reaching us, they focussed on me out
of the corner of their eye not saying a word;
then they turned to each other, and said:

"He seems alive from his throat's action;
but if they are dead, by what privilege
are they free of wearing the heavy stole?".

Then to me: "Oh Tuscan, who comes
to the congregation of sad hypocrites,
do not despise telling us who you are".

And I to them: "I was born and bred
by the lovely river Arno's main city,
and have the body I've always had.

But who are you, down whose cheeks
from what I see much sorrow pours?
and what sin is yours that so shines?".

One answered me: "the orange mantles
are so laden with lead, that their weight
makes us moan as do creaking scales.

We were *frati gaudenti*, natives of Bologna;
my name was Catalano and his Loderingo,
named and jointly appointed by your city

to what is normally entrusted to one man,
to maintain the peace; and such were we:
rubble still remains visible near Gardingo".

I began: "Oh friars, your transgressions…";
but stopped, because one crucified to
the ground by three stakes struck my eye.

On seeing me, his body contorted,
angrily snorting through his beard;
and friar Catalan, upon noticing it,

said: "That transfixed one you see,
counselled the Pharisees better one
be sacrificed for sake of the people.

Naked is he laid across the pathway,
as you see, and so is obliged to feel
the weight of all crossing passers-by.

So too is his father in law stretched out
in this pit, and the others of the council
who were the wicked seed for the Jews".

Then I saw Virgil marvel as to the
one stretched out upon a cross so
ignominiously in that eternal exile.

Then he directed these words to the friar:
"may it not displease you, if allowed, tell
us if on the right side there is an opening

by which we are able to exit from here,
without obliging any of the dark angels
to come and extract us from this depth".

He responded: "Closer than you think
goes a bridge from the large outer wall
stretching over all the horrifying bolge,

Canto XXIII

but is collapsed here and does not over-
arch; you can climb up the ruins against
the slope that are piled up from its base".

The guide stood a little with head down;
then said: "he that hooks the sinners
there falsely explained this situation".

And the friar: "I once heard in Bologna
of the devil's many vices, among which I
heard he is a liar, and father of all lies".

To which the guide left in long strides,
with a touch of anger on his expression;
so at this point I left the ladened ones

following the steps left by those dear feet.

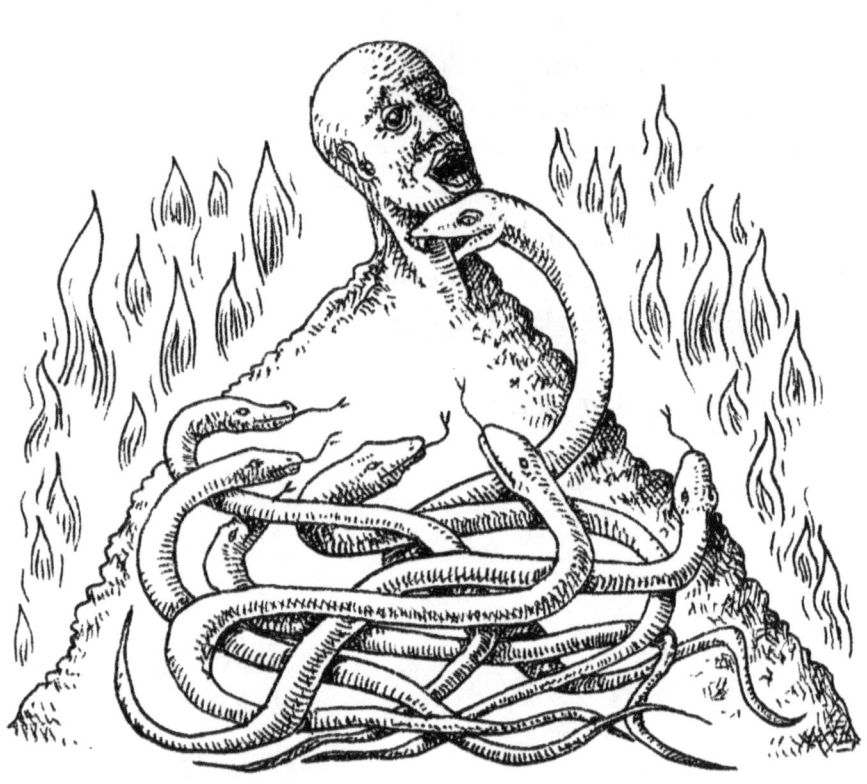

Canto XXIV

Virgil's anger converts once again to benevolence towards Dante as he elevates him and supports him during the climb of the extreme rocky slope. Notwithstanding, the climb is arduous and upon reaching the top, the pilgrim must sit down for his earthly body to recover. Virgil strongly challenges him to dispense with the urge to indulge in this as there is more demanding effort ahead. Dante spurs himself on along the more rugged ridge and perceives the voice of one moved by anger. Unable to see or hear clearly, the travellers descend the ridge to a horrific sight of snake infestation in the next bolgia. Here souls are compelled to fruitlessly run to avoid the snakes while these have bound their thieving hands. One of them is suddenly bitten in the neck and instantly catches fire, collapsing into a pile of ashes. He is then immediately reconstituted into his original form. His name is Vanni Fucci, whom Dante knows by his reputation for violence, who is relegated here for theft from the church sacristy which was attributed to an innocent person. To repay Dante for having discovered him, he prophesises bad tidings for Florence.

Dante's Inferno

At the onset of the new year when
the sun tempers its cold locks under
Aquarius and nights near half a day,

when frost on the ground duplicates
the image of its snow white sister,
but its pen's sharpness dissipates,

the peasant that is lacking in feed,
gets up, looks round, and sees fields
all whitened; so he slaps his thigh,

he returns home, grumbling to and fro,
as a wretch who knows not what to do;
then goes out again and regains hope,

seeing the world having changed face
in such short time, and takes his staff
and drives his sheep out to pasture.

In the same way as my Master dismayed
me when I saw him frowning in that way,
so too a quick remedy reached my wound;

for just as we came to the ruined bridge,
my guide turned with sweet countenance
that I first saw at the foot of the mount.

Opening his arms, he deliberated
first having examined the ruins
for the best way, and took me up.

And like one acting whilst evaluating,
always in preparation for next action,
so was he pushing me to the peak of

Canto XXIV

a large boulder, eye on another ledge
saying: "grip onto that one next; but
first check if it can bear your weight".

It wasn't a trek to be wearing a mantle:
he weightless and I being pushed could
hardly climb one rocky edge to another.

And if the slope of the enclosure had not
been shorter than the previous one, I know
not about him, but I'd have come undone.

But as Malebolge declines towards
the opening of the deepest of wells,
the position of each valley is such

that one bank is taller than the next; we
finally reached the top of the bank from
where the last rock had come detached.

My lungs were so drained of any breath
when I got to the top, I could not go on,
indeed barely upon arrival I sat down.

"Now you must be free of this sloth",
said Master: "as reclining on feathers or
under a bed cover cannot lead to fame;

without which he who wastes his life,
leaves the same remnant of himself,
as smoke in the air or froth on water.

Therefore get up; win over weariness
with a soul that wins all of its battles,
unless conceding to its body weight.

It is necessary to climb even longer stairs;
it not being enough to depart from these.
Benefit from this, if you grasp my meaning".

I then got up, and displaying as having
greater breathing than I actually did,
said: "Go, as I am strong and ardent".

We began walking along the ridge,
which was rocky, narrow and awkward,
and far steeper than the previous one.

I spoke while advancing to not appear
feeble; then came a voice from the next
ditch whose sounds lacked articulation.

I don't know what he said, though I was
at the peak of the arch that crosses over;
but his speech seemed driven by anger.

I was leaning down, but my mortal eyes
could not see the base for the darkness;
so I said: "Master, ensure you arrive at

the next bank and let us descend the wall;
because, as I hear but cannot comprehend,
so too looking down cannot discern a thing".

He said: "I do not respond other than by
my doing so, as such a legitimate request
must be satisfied in silence with action".

We descended the bridge to the extremity
where it joins the bank of the eighth pit,
so the bolgia was then laid out before me:

Canto XXIV

and in it I saw a terrible den of snakes,
and of such horrid species that still the
memory freezes the blood in my veins.

Lybia can't now brag about its sands;
notwithstanding the chelydri, jaculi,
phareans, cenchres and amphisbenes,

it never revealed any such pestiference
or toxicity even combining all Ethiopia
and the lands lying above the Red Sea.

In this cruel and ghastly plethora
ran naked and terrified people with
no hope of a hovel or a bloodstone:

hands tied behind their backs by snakes;
heads and tails pushed through kidneys,
entwining themselves onto their bellies.

Suddenly a serpent attacked one at
our embankment piercing him right
where the neck meets the shoulder,

Neither the letter 'O' nor 'I' were ever
written so quickly as his igniting, burning,
and completely collapsing into ashes;

and shortly after being thus annihilated
the ashes gathered unto themselves
immediately returning his original form.

So too as manifested by the great sages
the phoenix dies and is quickly reborn
approaching her five hundredth year;

Dante's Inferno

in life she doesn't feed on grasses or grain
but only tears of incense and Amomum,
and nard and myrrh compose her shroud.

As he that collapses not knowing how,
demonic possession dragging him down,
or by some occlusion that impedes him,

when upon rising, peers around
bewildered by the great distress
suffered, and looking on pants:

so was this sinner having gotten up.
Oh how severe, is the power of God,
wielding such blows as just revenge!

My guide then asked him who he was;
he replied: "I pelted down from Tuscany,
a short time ago, to this ferocious gorge.

I enjoyed a life beastly rather than human,
illegitimate that I was; I am Vanni Fucci
the beast, and Pistoia was my proper den".

I to my guide: "Tell him he is not to evade,
and ask which sin drove him down here;
as I knew him a man of bloodlust and fury".

And the sinner grasping it, did not fail
but to turn his spirit and eyes to me,
flushed with an angry sense of shame;

then he said: "I am more sorry you have
found me out in the misery you see me in,
than when snatched from the other life.

Canto XXIV

I cannot deny you that which you ask;
I am located lower down because I had
stolen treasured works from a sacristy,

and another was falsely accused of theft.
But so you cannot rejoice seeing me here,
if you ever make it out of the dark places,

open your ears to my prophecy, and listen.
Pistoia will divest itself of the Black party;
then Florence will alter people and modes.

Mars will draw a bolt from Val di Magra
that will be enveloped by thunderclouds;
with a ferocious and bitter tempest

will a battle occur over Campo Picen;
and the bolt will disperse the cloud,
so wounding each of the White party.

And I've said this so you endure pain!".

Canto XXV

Cursing, Vanni Fucci raises his hands in a profane gesticulation at God Himself whereupon he is attacked by snakes that respond by constricting his neck and binding his arms. Silenced and bound he exits, escaping the arrival of the centaur Cacus who, also guilty of fraud, is covered in snakes, carrying a dragon that breathes fire and is searching for him. Immediately, three spirits arrive trying to find Cianfa Donati who soon comes in the form of a six legged reptile that attacks the soul of Agnello Brunelleschi. He latches onto Agnello and the two fuse into a monstrous figure. This is followed by the advent of Guercio Cavalcanti in the form of a small snake that bites Buoso degli Abati and the two exchange forms. Only Puccio Sciancato is left unscathed at the end.

With these as his final words, the thief
lifted his fists on high in the form of figs,
shouting: "Take this, God, they're yours!".

From then on snakes became dear to me,
for one wrapped itself around his neck,
as if saying "you won't say anything else";

and another on his arms, tying him again,
entwining itself so tightly at his front,
he could not even twitch them.

Oh Pistoia, Pistoia why don't you resolve
to self immolate to cease existing, as you
exceed the evil actions of your ancestry?

In all hell's circles' darkness I never saw
a spirit this arrogant towards God, even
he that fell from the walls of Thebes.

He took off unable to utter a word;
and I saw arrive a centaur full of fury
shouting: "Where, where's the cruel one?".

I don't think Maremma has as many
snakes as did he on his back reaching
as far as where the human part begins.

On his shoulders, behind the nape
sat a dragon with opened wings;
combusting whomever it encounters.

My Master said: "This is Cacus, who,
at the grotto under Mount Aventine,
did often there create a lake of blood.

Canto XXV

He does not travel his brothers' road,
for the fraudulent theft committed
of the large herd located nearby;

for which his wicked actions ended under
Hercules' club, that maybe gave a hundred
blows, of which he could not feel the tenth".

While still speaking, Cacus made off,
and three spirits arrived beneath us,
which neither I nor my guide noticed,

had they not yelled: "Who are you?";
at which our conversation stopped,
and our attention diverted to them.

I did not know them; but it occurred,
as it does happen occasionally, that
one needed to call another by name,

saying: "What has happened to Cianfa?";
so that I, ensuring the Master's attention,
placed my finger on my chin to my nose.

If you now, reader, are slow to believe
what I am about to say, it is no surprise,
as I who did see it, am at pains to do so.

As I had my eye fixed upon them,
a reptile with six legs throws itself
upon one, latching on completely.

With its middle legs it clutched his belly
and with its front ones seized his arms;
then it mauled one cheek and the other;

its hind legs extended onto his thighs,
and placing its tail between his legs
it stretched it all the way up his back.

Never did ivy so cling to a tree
as did that horrifying creature
entwine its limbs around his.

Then they melded, as if made of hot wax,
their colours blending together, neither
one nor other appearing as it was before:

as does a piece of paper in the same way,
slowly darken before burning and it is
not yet black while the white dies away.

The other two observed him, and each
yelled: "Oh Agnel, how you're changing!
Look you are now neither two nor one".

Their two heads had already become one
when there appeared two blurred images
in one face into which both had been lost.

The four limbs had become two arms;
thighs with legs, and belly and chest
became members never before seen.

Every original feature became annulled:
the perverse image resembling the two
and neither; and in this way edged away.

As a green lizard under the sun's lashing
on scorchers, going one hedge to another
as lightning when it is crossing the road,

Canto XXV

so too seemed a flaming little snake
bruised black as peppercorn nearing
the bellies of the other two; and

he pierced one of them at the point
where as unborns we get nutrition;
then fell stretched out before him.

The pierced one looked on, saying nothing;
indeed, with feet immobile he yawned
as if overcome by sleep or by a fever.

He stared at the snake and it stared back;
intense smoke issued, from one's wound
and the other's mouth, the plumes merging.

Lucan must be silent in his reference
to the sad Sabellus and to Nasidius,
and attentive to what I now unleash.

Ovid must be silent of Cadmus and Arethusa,
that if in verse does transform he to serpent
and she to a fountain, I do not envy him;

he never placed two natures face to face
that transmuted so that each form was
inclined to exchange physical substance.

They both conformed in line with this,
the serpent's tail split becoming forked,
and the wounded one's feet merged.

His legs and thighs each conjoined so
quickly there was no evidence at all
one could see a join between them.

Dante's Inferno

The divided tail absorbed the human form
being lost by the other, and while its skin
was softening, the other's was hardening.

I saw his arms shrink back to the armpits,
and the beast's front legs, that were short,
grow as far as the others that had shrunk.

Then the rear legs, intertwining,
formed the part that man hides,
while the sinner's grew to two.

Then as the smoke enveloped each
in new colour, and generated hair
on one and depilation of the other,

one rose erect and the other fell down,
each not shifting their mutual evil eye,
below which snouts were transforming.

The erect one's retracted to the temples,
and from the excess flesh accumulated,
protruded ears and cheeks hereto absent;

of that which was not absorbed back in,
the residual formed the nose on its face
and lips to the point of natural size.

The one supine lengthened its snout,
withdrawing its ears back to the head
as does the snail with its antennae.

and his tongue, that was singular and ready
for speech, split in two, and the other's
biforked one closed; and the smoke ends.

Canto XXV

The soul that had become a reptile,
made off into the valley hissing, with
the other behind speaking and spitting.

Then turning his new shoulders around,
he said to the other: "I want Buoso to run,
as I have, on all fours along this road".

So I saw the refuse of the seventh alter
and transmutate, and may its unique-
ness excuse a slight straying of my pen.

And as much as my eyes were a little
confused and my soul disorientated,
they could not escape unnoticed,

preventing my clearly recognising Puccio
Sciancato of the earlier three, the only
one that did not metamorphose;

the other was the one you mourn, Gaville.

Canto XXVI

Dante the author rails against the Florence and its thievery exemplified in the five examples of citizens from the previous Canto. He and Virgil commence their climb of the slope that took them there to then arrive where he observes a multitude of single flames in the deep pit. Each flame contains a soul within it. Virgil points out one of them that has a dual tip and explains that it has the souls of Odysseus and Diomed in it. Although Dante wishes to engage them in conversation, Virgil asserts that he himself should speak to them implying that he has the commensurate status of being an ancient poet. Odysseus responds to Virgil's highly formalised introduction of himself, explaining who he is with reference to the events in Homer's Odyssey. Odysseus describes how, having exceeded the Pillars of Hercules, a wind descended upon the ship, sealing their fate.

Dante's Inferno

Rejoice, Florence, as you are so great
your wings flap over sea and 'scape,
and your name extends across hell!

Among the thieves I found five of
your shameful so noble citizens,
nor are you honourably elevated.

But if closer to morning dreams are true,
you will feel, shortly from now, what
Prato, amongst others, do threaten you.

If it already were, it would not be too early.
If only it had come to pass, as it must do so!
As the more I age, the more it is insufferable.

We went off, and up by those steps
of protruding spurs of earlier descent,
Master climbing, drawing me along;

and proceeding on the solitudinous path,
amongst the splinters and ridge's spikes,
feet not advancing without using hands.

I then felt sorrow, and still feel sorrowful
in turning my mind to what I witnessed,
and I restrain my insight more than usual,

so it travels not without virtue as its guide;
that, if a lucky star or something greater first
gave me this gift, I do not deprive myself of it.

Just as a peasant on the hillside rests,
in the season when he that brightens
the world keeps his face from us less,

Canto XXVI

when the fly concedes to the mosquito,
sees the many fireflies down in the valley,
maybe where he harvests grapes and plows:

so too did as many flames glow
in the eighth bolgia, as I saw
from where the base was visible.

As he who avenged himself with bears
witnessing Elijah's chariot's ascension,
when the horses shot up into the sky,

unable to follow him with his gaze,
seeing no more than a single flame,
which ascended like a small cloud:

so does each move in the bowels
of the pit, none displaying the theft,
and each flame a sinner conceals.

I was erect on the bridge looking out,
so if I hadn't grasped a rocky protrusion,
I'd have without a nudge fallen down.

And my guide seeing me so engrossed,
said: "Inside of those flames are spirits;
each enveloped by that which burns it".

"Master", replied I, "in listening to you
I am more certain; but I had seen that
it was so, and had planned to ask you:

who is it within the fire that bifurcates
at its tip, so from the pyre that Etèocles
and brother were lain on seems to rise?".

He replied: "Within there are tormented
Ulysses and Diomed, being so together
under just revenge as had been in wrath;

and within their flame they suffer for the
deception of the horse opening the door
from which came the noble Roman seed.

They also suffer for the deceit by which
though dead, Deidamia still mourns Achilles,
and punishment incur for the Palladium.

"If they within those flames can speak",
I said: "Master, much I pray, and pray on
my prayer so it multiply a thousand fold,

that you do not prevent me to wait
on the horned flame coming here;
see how passion inclines me to it!".

And he to me: "Your prayer is deserving
of much praise, and I therefore accept it;
but ensure that you hold your tongue.

Let me do the talking, because I fathom
what you want; and having been Greek,
they could disdain listening to your words".

After the flame arrived at a point seeming
opportune in time and place to my guide,
this is the manner I heard him speak in:

"Oh you two held in the one flame,
if I were worthy to you while alive,
if I were worthy of much or of little

Canto XXVI

while on earth writing noble verses,
do not leave; but one of you do tell
where in getting himself lost, he died".

The higher tip of the ancient flame
began fluttering and murmuring
as if buffeted by a blustering wind;

then, tip flicking this way and that,
as if a tongue were in fact speaking,
it spoke up and said: "When

I departed from Circe, who detained
me more than one year near Gaeta,
before Eneas gave such a name to it,

neither sweetness of son, nor devotion
to an aging father, nor the love due
that would have made Penelope happy,

could win against the ardour I had
within to gain worldly experience
of humanity's vices and its virtue;

but I placed myself on the high seas
with only a ship and that company
of few men which did not desert me.

I saw one shore to another as far as Spain,
and Morocco and the island of Sardinia,
and the other shores washed by that sea.

My mates and I were old and weak
when we came to that narrow strait
where Hercules set his boundaries

beyond which man can go no further;
on the right hand side I went by Seville,
on the left I had earlier left Ceuta.

O brothers', I said: 'who after a hundred
thousand perils have arrived at the west,
in this such a small phase of awareness

that still remains available to our senses,
don't deprive yourselves the experience of
following the sun, to the world uninhabited.

Consider the origins of your seed:
not made to live as though brutes,
but to pursue virtue and knowledge'.

I rendered my companions so desirous
for the journey, with my brief discourse,
that at pains could have held them back;

and turning our stern to face the dawn,
made wings of the oars in a flight of folly,
always gaining distance to the left.

At night I beheld all stars of the other
pole, and our hemisphere was so low
it did not emerge above the horizon.

Five times the bottom lunar hemisphere
came alight and was then extinguished,
after we embarked on the hard journey,

when a mount appeared to us, indistinct
due to the distance, that seemed higher
than any other I had ever seen before.

Canto XXVI

We cheered up, but quickly turned to tears;
as from that new land was born a whirl-
wind that struck the prow of the ship.

Three times it turned the ship in a vortex;
and on the fourth it lifted the stern high
and sent the prow low, as pleased Another,

until the ocean above closed over us".

Canto XXVII

The scene of the previous Canto ends with poignant silence as the flame, now still, receives Virgil's dispensation to leave. Another flame directly behind it approaches. Its soul addressing Virgil because it hears his Lombard, requests information on the political situation in Italy. This time Virgil urges Dante to speak as the soul is of an Italian. Dante gives his outline of various cities and then urges the soul to identify itself. It is reluctant to but being convinced Dante will not be returning above, reveals it is the soul of Guido da Montefeltro who had been a soldier and repented of his sins later in life, becoming a friar. His sin as a friar that led to his damnation came as a military strategist in giving false counsel to Pope Boniface VIII. At the point of death, a demon came and in employing logic, successfully lay claim to his soul.

Dante's Inferno

The flame was now motionless and straight
as it had no more left to say, and as it left
on receiving licence to by the gentle poet,

did another, coming up behind it
draw our eyes upwards to its tip
for the confused sound escaping it.

As the Sicilian bull bellowed first
with cry of he, and this was just,
that had as its artisan created it,

bellowing with the inner afflicted's voice,
such that, though made entirely of brass,
it seemed stabbed by pain nevertheless;

so, when at first not having an outlet
or opening through the fire, his desperate
words sounded as if a flame did make.

But after having found a way of issuing
up through the tip, having the flicking
action the tongue had now given it,

we heard: "Oh you to whom I direct
my voice and who just spoke Lombard,
saying 'Now go, I exhort you no more',

though I arrive perhaps with tardiness,
may it not displease you to talk to me;
see it displeases me not, though I burn!

If you only just fell into this blind
world from that sweet Italian land
from which all my sin doth derive,

Canto XXVII

tell me if Romagnoles have peace or war;
as I was from mountains between Urbino
and the range wherefrom is released the Tiber".

I was still attentively leaning when
my guide lightly elbowed my side,
saying: "Speak, this one is Italian".

And I who had a ready response,
began speaking without hesitation:
"Oh soul that is down there hidden,

Your Romagna is not, and never was
without war in the heart of its tyrants;
but as I left just now there was none.

Ravenna is as it has been for many years:
the eagle of the Da Polenta hovers over it,
so as to stretch over Cervia with its wings.

The city that withstood the long trial
and of the French made a bloody pile,
falls again under the lion's green claws.

The old Verrucchian mastiff and its younger
that subjected Montagna to mistreatment,
continue to maul there as always have done.

The cities of Lamone and Santerno are
ruled by the lion of the white lair who
shifts alliances from one day to the next.

And that city's side the Savio does bathe,
being between mountain and the plain,
also lives next to tyranny as a free state.

Dante's Inferno

Now I pray you tell us who you are;
don't be more resistant than others, so
your earthly fame may hold its head high".

After the fire had roared for a while in its
usual way, the sharp point moved side
to side, and so breathed out this sound:

"If I thought that my reply would be to he
who sooner or later would return to earth,
this flame would remain without a flicker;

however as no one from this depth
has ever returned alive, if it be truth,
I reply without fear of defamation.

I was a man of arms, then Franciscan Friar,
thinking to amend by donning the cord:
and it would have been the case, if not

for the High Priest, to hell with him!
who led me to my earlier state of sin;
I want you to know the how and why.

While I was still made of flesh and blood
that my mother gave me, my works
were not leonine, but rather of a fox.

I knew all of the strategies and covert
methods, and so well practised the art,
my fame echoed to the four corners of earth.

When I saw I had arrived at that
stage of life when each should
lower sails and pull in the lines,

Canto XXVII

what earlier pleased me, caused remorse;
repentant and confessed, I took the call;
oh dear! It could to my benefit have been.

The prince of the new Pharisees,
engaging in war at the Lateran,
and not against Saracen nor Jew,

as each enemy was Christian, and
none had conquered Acre nor was
trading arms in the Sultan's land,

neither his high office nor holy orders
did hold in regard, nor the cord I wore
that used to keep its wearers slim.

Instead as Constantine sent for Silvestro
from within Soracte to heal his leprosy,
so he called on me to be his physician

to heal him from his feverish pride; he
asked my counsel, and I was dumbstruck
as his words seemed those of a drunk.

He then said: "Let your heart not fear;
Of this sin I now absolve you, teach me
how I can raze Praeneste to the ground.

I lock and unlock the Kingdom of Heaven,
as you know; because two are the keys
which my predecessor did not hold dear".

So, authoritative argument persuaded
me as remaining silent seemed graver,
and I: "Father, given you absolve me

of that sin into which I must now fall,
promising much while delivering little
will make you triumphant on the throne".

St. Francis then came at my point of death
to collect me; but one of the black cherubim
told him: 'Do not take him: do not deny me.

He must come down among my lackeys
because he did give fraudulent counsel,
over which I've had him by the short and curlies since;

as forgiveness cannot be for the unrepentant,
nor can repentance and desire to sin co-exist
as the contradiction in terms doesn't allow it'.

Oh poor me! How shocked I was
when he took me saying: 'Perhaps
you did not think I was a logician'.

Before Minos he took me; and he curled
his tail around his hard back eight times;
and then having bitten it in a fit of rage,

held: 'he is of they whom the fire steals';
so here I am, lost as you can see me,
and clothed as such, proceed, lamenting".

When he had finished speaking thus,
the sorrowing flame then departed,
twisting and flicking its sharp horn.

We went further, both I and my guide,
up the bridge onto the next arch that
covers the pit where pay the levy they

who in disuniting, gained their load.

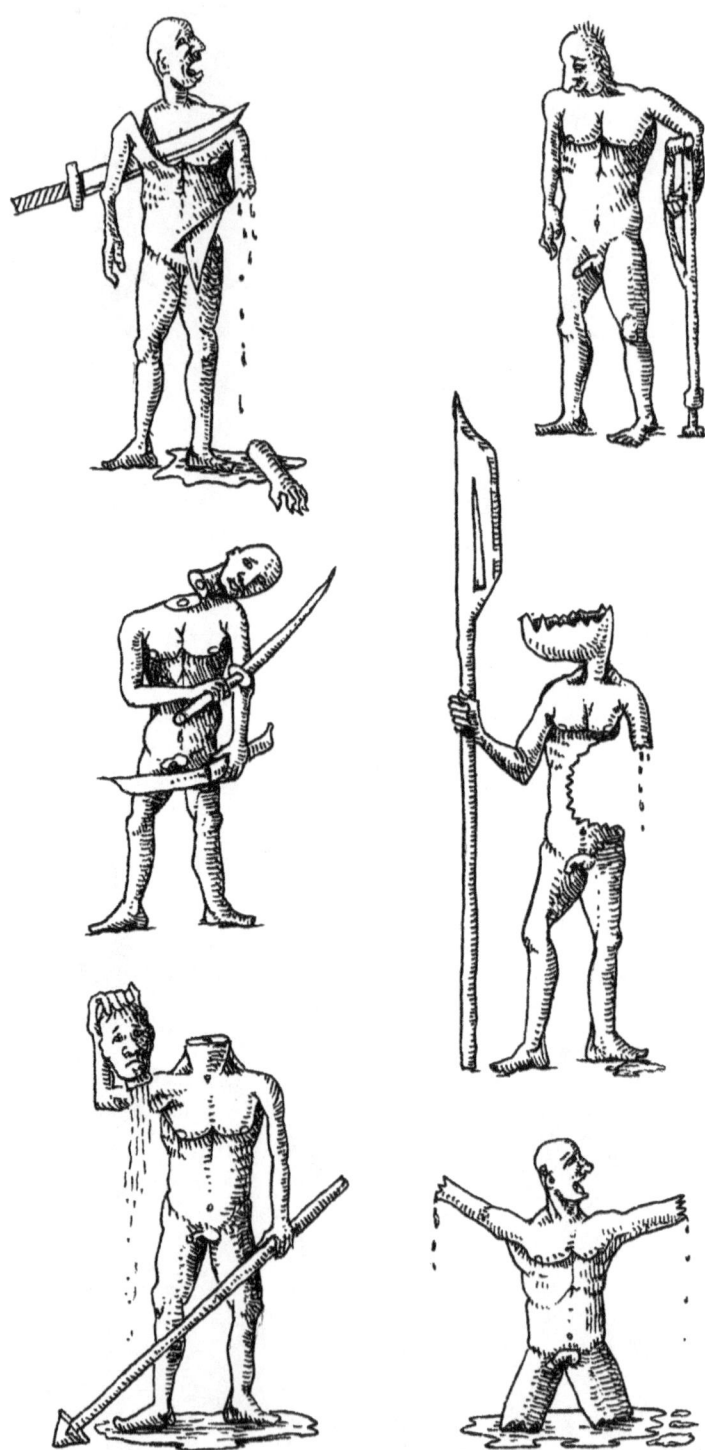

Canto XXVIII

The extremity of what Dante the pilgrim witnesses in this Canto leads him to portray it with reference to historical extremes of military slaughter. This ninth bolgia contains those who caused scandal and schism, and the torment they are subject to reflects division in the literal sense that is meted out on their bodies. Personages of note subject to the butchering are: Mahomet, Ali, Pier da Medicina, Galus Scribonius Curio, Mosca de' Lamberti, Bertran de Born and Pier da Medicina.

Dante's Inferno

Who could ever even by using prose
fully narrate of the blood and wounds
I now saw, though re-telling many times?

Any tongue would certainly fall short
due to our language and our intellect
having little scope to contain so much.

Even if we gathered all the people
who once, upon the fateful terrain
of Puglia, having been martyred

because of the Romans and long conflict
that produced such large booty of rings,
as writes Livy, whose account doesn't err,

along with those mortally struck
while opposing Robert Guiscard;
and others whose bones still lie

at Ceperano, there where each Puglian
betrayed, and near Tagliacozzo, where
old Alardo won without use of arms;

even if all compared members pierced
and amputated, it could never equate to
the lurid conditions of the ninth bolgia.

A wine barrel losing a midboard or cant,
would not appear as broken, as one I saw
split from chin to where wind breaks.

The entrails did hang between his legs;
vital organs showed as did the repugnant
pouch that makes excrement of food we eat.

Canto XXVIII

While I held my gaze totally upon him,
he looked, his hands parting his chest,
saying: "Now look how I splay myself!

Look how deformed Mahomet is!
Before me Alì goes about crying,
with face sliced chin to forelock.

And all the others you see in here,
were sowers of discord and schism
in life, and for that are cut this way.

There is a devil here who cleaves us
so cruelly, submitting each one of
this chapter to the sword's edge,

once we have rounded the dolorous path;
so the wounds have healed over again
ahead of reappearing before him.

But who are you musing on the bridge,
perhaps you delay going to your self-
confessed adjudicated punishment?".

My Master: "he is neither taken by death,
nor led by his sin to submit to torment;
but it is to give him full comprehension,

I, who am dead, must accompany him
down here through hell circle by circle;
this is as true as I presently talk to you".

Upon hearing it, more than one hundred
stopped in the pit to look straight at me
in amazement, forgetting their suffering.

"So you who may well soon see the sun,
do tell fra Dolcin unless he wish to soon
follow me here, to make provision

of victuals, so the impact of being snowed
in does not hand victory to the Novarese,
a thing not otherwise easy to achieve".

Having positioned his foot to leave,
Mahomet said these words to me;
then setting it down went his way.

Another one, with his throat slashed
and with nose cut up to his eyelashes,
and who had only but one ear left,

stood there in amazement looking on with
others, ahead of them he opened his throat,
that oozed vermilion from every part of it,

saying: "Oh you whom sin doesn't condemn
and whom I saw up above in the Latin land,
unless I am misled by your similar looks,

do remember me Pier da Medicina,
should you return to see sweet plains
that descend from Vercelli to Marcabò.

And tell the distinguished two in Fano,
the Messer Guido and also Angiolello,
that, if foreseeing here isn't fallacious,

due to a malicious tyrant's treachery
they, tied with weights, will be tossed
from their ship to drown near Cattolica.

Canto XXVIII

Neptune has never seen so great a crime
from the islands of Cyprus to Majorca,
neither by pirates nor by the Greeks.

That traitor who sees only out of one eye,
who governs land that one here near me
would rather had never cast his eye upon,

will call them to come and confer with him;
and will arrange so they will not need either
vows or prayers to avoid Focara's wind".

And I to him: "Identify and clarify who is
the one for whom the seeing was so bitter,
if you wish me to bring news of you above".

Then he placed his hand upon the jaw
of a companion and opened his mouth,
crying: "This is he, and he cannot speak.

He, when sent into exile, put paid to any
hesitation in Caesar, convincing that one
ready to act always suffers when delayed".

Oh how he seemed so shocked to me
with his tongue cut deep in his throat,
Curio, once so bold in his speaking!

And one whose hands were lopped off,
raising his stumps in the tenebrous air,
such that the blood smeared his face,

screamed: "You must also remember Mosca,
who said, sadly!, 'What's done is done',
which germinated discord for the Tuscans".

To which I said: "And ruin of your lineage";
by which, in adding salt to the wound,
he went off dejected and out of his mind.

But I remained looking at the throng,
and saw something that I would fear
without other testimony, to recount;

however my conscience reassures me:
the good companion that bolsters man,
under the chain mail of feeling pure.

I saw clearly, and it appears I still see,
a headless body going the same way
as the others of that miserable flock;

and he held his severed head by the hair,
it hanging from one hand as if a lantern:
and he looked at us saying: "Oh dear me!".

He made a lamp of himself unto himself,
and the two were one and the one was two;
how so, only He decreeing all can know.

Once arrived right at the foot of the bridge,
he lifted his arm holding his head up high
to direct his words more closely to us,

which were: "See my horrid punishment,
you who, breathing, go visiting the dead:
see if there is one as extreme as mine.

And so that you may bring news of me,
know that I am Bertran de Born, he that
gave the young king perfidious counsel.

Canto XXVIII

I set father and son against each other;
Achitophel wasn't any worse in malicious
incitement of Absalom and David.

Because I divided such conjoined people,
I am constrained, alas!, to carry my brain,
severed from its source in this my bust.

In me you see punishment befitting the crime".

Canto XXIX

The Canto begins with Virgil scolding Dante for his obsessive focus on those in the pit. Dante replies that he was doing so as he thought he could see a relative of his among the sinners. Virgil confirms that he had already noted this soul, Geri del Bello, who was pointing at Dante threateningly and who gave up doing so because Dante was engrossed in observing the Lord of Hautefort. Dante is disturbed by the event and tells Virgil it is because Geri's violent death has not yet been avenged by those that are bound to do so by vicarious responsibility i.e. family members. Such retribution was a feature of Tuscan society of his time. The travellers converse until they reach the circle of the falsifiers. Here they see human figures strewn on the ground in a disordered way. They come to Griffolino d'Arezzo and Capocchio who are frantically scraping leprous scabs from their bodies. These relay how they came to their damnation by false words and false metals.

Dante's Inferno

The multitude and strange wounds
had inebriated my eyes so much,
that they were inclined to weep.

But Virgil said: "What engrosses you?
that causes your eye to become fixed
down there on the amputated sinners?

You didn't behave so in the other bolge;
consider, if you are thinking to count them,
the valley circumference is twenty two miles.

And already the moon is below our feet;
the time allocated to us is now short,
and there's more that you don't now see".

"If you had", I immediately replied,
"heeded the reason I was looking,
maybe you'd have let me remain longer".

Meanwhile, my guide was leaving
and I following ready with a reply
and adding: "Within that bolgia on

which I had fixed my eyes, I think a spirit
from my own bloodline was weeping for
the sin that is so costly down there".

Then my Master said: "Do not be
bothered over him from hereon in.
Think beyond it, and leave him be;

because I saw him under our small bridge
pointing you out and cursing menacingly,
and I heard him be called Geri del Bello.

Canto XXIX

You were then so entirely engrossed
with he who once held Hautefort,
that you didn't look his way, so he left".

"Oh my guide, his violent death that
has not as yet been avenged", I said,
"by others also bound by the offence,

made him disdainful; for which as I see he
distanced himself from me without a word,
for this reason I am more moved by him".

So we talked to the point on the bridge first
allowing a view all the way to the bottom
of the next bolgia, had there been more light.

When we arrived over the Malebolge's
final cloister, so that its brotherhood
were able to be visually evident to us,

I was struck by terrible moaning, piercing
me as steel tipped arrows arousing my pity;
at which I covered my ears with my hands.

The same moaning that would occur if
from July to September, the hospital sick
of Maremma, Valdichiana, and Sardinia

were all brought together in one ditch,
so too here, and with stench as does
come from decomposing members.

We descended from the long ridge
onto the last bank, keeping to the left;
and it was then the view was clearer

Dante's Inferno

down to the bottom where justice,
ministress of Divine infallibility
punishes her noted counterfeiters.

I don't think a sadder event was seen
in Aegina where all people were struck ill,
when the air became so full of pestilence,

that animals, down to the smallest insect,
all fell, and then the ancient inhabitants,
according to affirmation by the poets,

were derived again from the ants;
as it was seeing spirits languishing
in piles within that gloomy bolgia.

Some on others' bellies, some on the
shoulders of another, and some dragging
on all fours along the base of the bolgia.

We walked slowly without speaking,
looking and listening to the ill ones,
that could not get off the ground.

I saw two sitting leaning on each other,
in the way saucepans heat side by side,
marked with scabs from head to toe;

never did I see a currycomb move as quickly
by stable boy keeping his master waiting,
nor he that is reluctantly working a vigil,

than each one continuously scratching
themselves with their nails because of
the intense itch, that has no other relief;

Canto XXIX

and their nails scraped off scabs
as does a knife scale a bream
or other fish having larger scales.

"You whose fingers undo your chainmail",
began my guide addressing one of them,
"and at times use them as if were pliers,

tell us if an Italian is among those
in this place, and may your nails
last you eternally in this effort".

"We whom you see so decrepit
are both Italians", said one crying;
"but who are you asking after us?".

And the guide said: "I am one descending
circle by circle with this one who is living,
and am intent on showing him inferno".

At which ended their mutual leaning;
and trembling each turned towards me
along with others that had overheard.

The good Master directed his focus to me,
saying: "tell them whatever you wish";
and I began, as he had wished it to be:

"May the memory of you not fade
from human minds on the earth,
but may it live under many suns,

Tell me who you are and of your origins;
may your disfiguring and repulsive pains
not cause reluctance to reveal yourselves to me".

"I was native of Arezzo, and Albert of Siena",
answered one: "had me burned alive; but
that for which I died is not why I am here.

In truth, I had said to him in jest:
'I know how to fly through the air';
and he, with curiosity but little insight,

wanted me to show him the art; and just
because I did not change him to Daedalus,
had me burned by he who saw him as a son.

But into the last of the ten bolge for
the alchemy I had practised on earth
damned me Minos, who does not err".

I said to the poet: "has there ever been
a people more foolish than the Sienese?
Even the French fail to compare".

At which the other leper, who heard me,
replied: "Among those exclude Stricca
who knew how to moderate his spending,

and Niccolò who first discovered
costly use of cloves in the orchard
where the seed is wont to take root;

and exclude those in whose company Caccia
d'Ascian squandered vines and great holdings,
and Abbagliato put his intellect on show.

But so you know who is on your side
against the Sienese, fix your eye on me,
so my face may well reveal who I am:

Canto XXIX

you will see that I am the soul of Capocchio,
who falsified metals by using alchemy;
and you will recall, if I remember you truly,

how well I aped the things of nature".

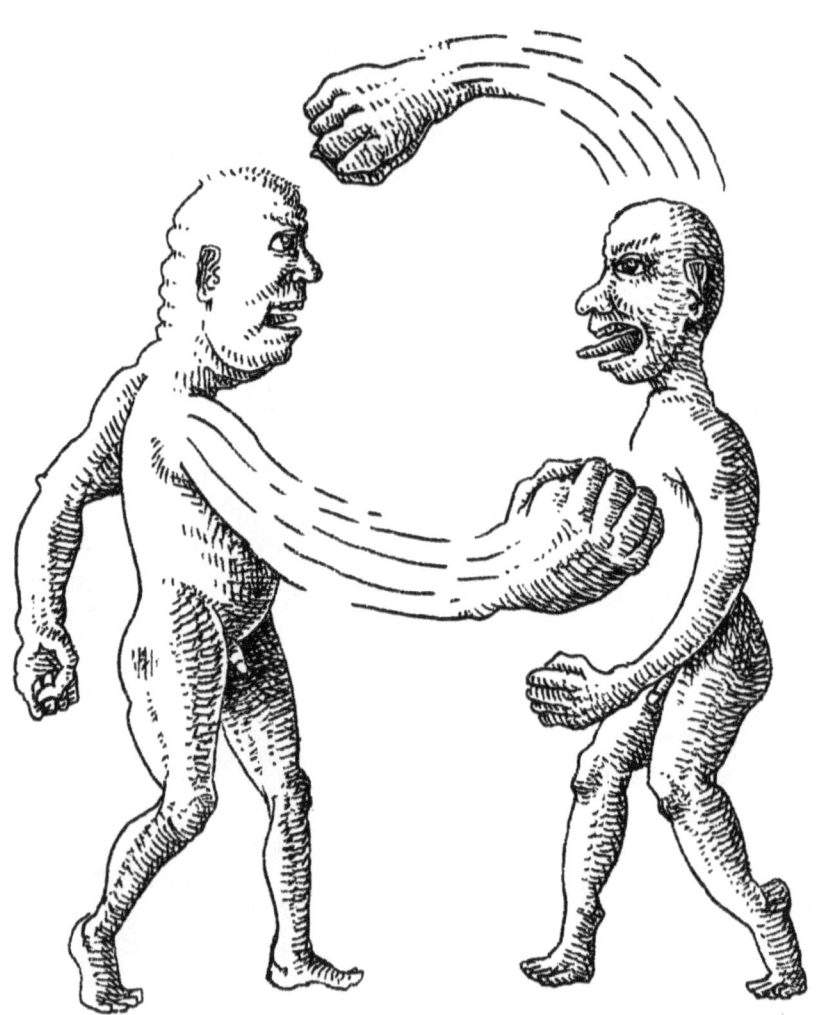

Canto XXX

In this Canto, violence, rage and madness suddenly occur when two naked souls appear and one of them, Gianni Schicchi, bites Capocchio on the neck and drags him off along the stoney ground. The other one is identified by Griffolino as the incestuous mythological figure, Myrrha of Cyprus. Next, Dante encounters Master Adamo a counterfeiter whose misshapen body constantly craves water. Dante asks about the two figures nearby and Master Adamo relates disparagingly that they are Potiphar's wife and Sinon the Greek. The latter strikes him with his fist and he responds in kind. This leads to a circuitous verbal exchange between them which Dante entertains only to attract the Virgil's reproach. This is retracted upon Dante's instinctive embarrassment at his own indulgence.

Dante's Inferno

At the time when Juno was enraged
as she had been on previous occasions,
at the Theban bloodline due to Semele,

Athamas went mad to the point,
that seeing his wife coming along
carrying a son in each of her arms,

screamed: "Let us cast the nets so I can
capture the lioness and cubs mid-flight";
and then stretched out his cruel talons,

seizing the one that was named Learco,
spinning him round dashing him on a rock;
she drowning herself with her other load.

And when Fortune's wheel turned
against Trojan daring's atrocities,
so kingdom and king were defeated,

Hecuba, anguished, miserable and enslaved,
after she saw that Polyxena was dead,
and the grieving one saw her Polydorus

was lying on the seashore, being
deranged she bayed like a dog;
such sorrow distorted her mind.

But neither Theban nor Trojan fury
was manifest at anyone so cruelly,
wounding animal, or human limb,

as the two spirits I saw pale and nude,
that were running and biting in the way
a pig does when let loose from the sty.

Canto XXX

One reached Capocchio and sank his teeth
into his nape, so much so, that in pulling,
he grated his belly along the hard surface.

And the Aretine left behind, trembling
said: "That gremlin is Gianni Schicchi,
and he furiously goes mauling others".

"Oh", I said, "may the other not sink
his teeth into you, if it pleases you
say who he is, before he goes away".

And he replied: "That is the ancient spirit
of Mirra the wicked, who became
her father's friend beyond licit love.

This is how she came to sin with him
by faking having another person's body
just like that one down there dared to,

who, to take the best mare of the herd,
falsified his identity as Buoso Donati,
as testator and gave a will legal form".

And after the two furious souls
I kept my eye on had departed,
I turned to the others born cursed.

I saw one who took the form of a lute,
had he been truncated below the groin
where a man's legs are forked.

The heavy dropsy, that due to humors
that do not convert deforms members
so the face is disproportionate to the belly,

caused him to keep his lips wide open
as does someone thirsty from a fever,
turning one lip up and the other down.

"Oh you who without punishment, and
I know not why, are in this grave world",
he said to us, "look and do take note

of the misery afflicting Master Adamo;
alive, I had more than I could wish for,
and now, alas!, crave a drop of water.

Those streamlets from the Casentino
green hills descending to the Arno,
making their riverbeds cool and soft

are always before me, not without effect,
as their memory makes me thirstier still
more that the illness emaciating my face.

The severe justice that torments me
draws from the place in which I sinned
provoking my sighing even further.

Therein lies Romena, where I forged coin
minted with the image of the Baptist;
for which I left my burned body above.

But if I could here see the miserable souls
of Guido or Alessandro or of their brother,
I would not exchange it for Fonte Branda.

One of them is already in here, if the raging
spirits running around do tell the truth;
but what use is that with my bound limbs?

Canto XXX

If I had been even a touch more agile
to move an inch every hundred years,
I would already be up and on my way,

to find him among these deformed people,
though this pit's circumference is eleven miles,
and is no less than a half mile across.

It is due to them that I am with such family;
it is they who induced me to mint florins
containing three carats of base metal".

And I said: "who are the two miserable ones
who give off steam as wet hands in winter,
lying tightly there to your right boundary?".

"They were here – when I plummeted into
this pit", he said, "and haven't turned since,
and I do not think they will do so ever.

It is she who did falsely accused Joseph;
the other is the liar Sinon Greek of Troy:
smelling so badly due to their high fever".

And one of them, who was annoyed
at being referred to so infamously,
struck the bloated belly with his fist.

And it made the sound of a drum;
and Master Adamo struck his face
with his arm, being of no less force,

saying to him: "Although I am denied
movement of my limbs that are heavy,
my arm is at the ready for such work".

To which he replied: "when you were sent
to burn at the stake, you weren't so quick;
but were this and more when you minted".

And the dropsical one: "You tell the truth:
but you were not so truthful a witness
when questioned on the truth at Troy".

Sinon replied: If I spoke falsely, you minted so,
and I am here for one sin, whereas
you are for more than any other demon!".

"Remember, perjurer, about the horse",
replied the one with the bloated belly;
"may it hurt you all the world knows!".

"And may the thirst cracking your tongue
hurt", said the Greek, "and foul humour bloat
your belly to a hedge blocking your eyes!".

Then the counterfeiter: "May your mouth
split open from your illness now as always;
so that, if I thirst and humour bloats me,

you burn and headaches hurt you,
and licking the mirror of Narcissus,
would not require much prompting".

I was there intent on listening to them,
when Master said: "go on, get your fill,
as I am not far off fighting with you!".

When I heard him speak with this anger,
I turned towards him with such shame,
that I still have it etched in my memory.

Canto XXX

As one dreaming a thing harmful to him,
though dreaming hopes it is only a dream,
ardently desiring what is, as if it were not,

so became I, unable to find the words,
because I wanted to apologise, but my
shame did so without my knowing it.

"Lesser shame than yours serves to wash",
an even greater sin," said the Master, "than
you committed, so abandon all remorse.

And act as if I am always at your side,
should luck have it that you are again
placed with spirits in a similar dogfight:

as having a taste for this is a base desire".

Canto XXXI

The travellers make their way out of the pit and through the dismal air. They then hear a thunderous blast of a horn which draws Dante's attention to tall constructs in the distance. As he approaches, Virgil explains they are in fact primordial giants. He names Nimrod, Ephialtes, Briareus, Tityus, Typhon and Antaeus who is the only one not to be in chains. The giants are embedded in the ground up to their waists and are therefore entirely immobile except Antaeus who, upon the request of Virgil, takes the travellers into his hand and lowers them onto the lake of ice below, which is the core of hell.

Dante's Inferno

The very tongue that first gave me a lashing,
making both one and other cheek blush,
did then hand unto me the medication;

thus did I hear the telling of how Achilles'
and his father's spear was wont to cause
first wounds and then a gratuitous gesture.

We turned our backs on the horrid valley
going over the embankment encircling it,
making our way across without a word.

'Twas not quite night and not quite day,
so my vision could not see much ahead;
but I heard a horn blow so potently,

as to make even thunder sound feeble,
that drew my eye to a particular point,
in the direction opposite to its source.

Even after the bloody defeat, when
Charlemagne lost the holy knights,
did Orlando not sound it so awfully.

I turned my head there for a short time,
where there seemed many high towers;
so I said: "Master, pray tell, what city is this?".

And he to me: "As you are viewing
from a long way away in this gloom,
what you imagine is confusing you.

If you do arrive there, you will realise,
how your sense can mislead from afar;
therefore hurry on more purposefully".

Canto XXXI

Then he took me kindly by the hand
and said: "Before we proceed further,
so that it seems less extraordinary,

know they are not towers, but giants,
positioned around the bank of the pit
and from the belly button down in it".

As when fog clears away and vision
gradually begins to focus upon that
hidden by a mist hanging in the air,

so my gaze traversed the dense dark air,
getting closer and closer to the pit's edge,
my error dissipating and my fear growing;

indeed, as Monteriggioni is encircled by
a crown of towers along its external wall,
so too this bank circumscribing the well

is towered over by half the body of
the horrible giants, whom Jove still
menaces from heaven by thundering.

And I could already distinguish one face,
shoulders, chest and much of the belly,
and both the arms down along his sides.

Certainly when Nature stopped creating
such beings as this, it did a good thing
because it denied Mars these forces.

And if she doesn't fear creating elephants
and whales, they who consider acutely,
will judge her even more just and prudent;

because when the faculty of reason
is added to corrupt will and passion,
people can have no defence against it.

His face looked as long and wide
as the Cone at St Peter's in Rome,
and his bones were proportional;

to the extent that the shore of the pit
acting as a loincloth from navel down
left such a height of the upper body

three Frisians end to end could not boast
of reaching his hair; as I saw he was thirty
hand spans high from cloak buckle down.

"Raphèl maí amècche zabí almi",
began crying the monstrous mouth,
that could not sustain sweeter songs.

And my guide responded: "Idiotic spirit,
hang onto that horn, and when gripped
by anger or other passion vent with it!

Feel round your neck, and you will find
the belt holding it, oh confused spirit,
and look how it lines your great chest".

Then he said to me: "He is a self accuser;
this is Nimrod by whose impious thought
one language is no longer spoken on earth.

Let's leave him be and not waste words;
as all the languages are unknown to him
as his to others, being incomprehensible".

Canto XXXI

We therefore continued with our walk,
to the left; and in an arbalest shot arrived
at another even larger and more ferocious.

I cannot say who the master craftsman was,
that chained him so, but he had his left arm
tied in front and his right arm tied behind

by a chain that held him bound from
the neck down, so that it wrapped him
five times across his visible upper body.

"This arrogant one wanted to compare
his strength with that of the supreme Jove",
said my guide, "so he has this reward.

Ephialtes by name, he cast a great challenge
when the giants impressed fear on the gods;
the arms he brandished, ever immobilised".

And I to him: "If possible, I'd like
to be able to cast my eye directly
upon the immense Briareus".

To which he replied: "You'll see Antaeus
near here who can speak and is loose,
who will put us down in the pit of all evil.

He whom you wish to see is much further on
and is fastened having a physique like this one,
but he is more ferocious in appearance".

Never was a quake so great,
that shook a tower so solid,
as Ephialtes' promptness to shake.

It was then I feared death more than ever,
and it would have been enough to finish me,
had it not been for the chains I beheld.

We then proceeded, and reached
Antaeus who, excluding his head rose
a good five ells beyond the pit wall.

"Oh you who in the fortunate valley
that rendered glory to Scipio, when
Hannibal and his men had retreated,

who took captive many lions as your prey,
and had you participated in the great war
along with your brothers, some still opine

the sons of the earth would have won:
place us down, and may you not disdain,
where the cold does freeze Cocytus.

Do not have us approach Tityus or Typhon:
he here can give that which is craved for:
so do incline and do not give us a wry look.

He can still render you fame on earth,
as he is alive, and has much longevity
but for Grace calling him ahead of time".

So spoke the Master; the other promptly
extended his hands, whose great strength
Hercules once felt, and he took my guide.

When Virgil felt himself taken hold of,
he said: "Come closer so I can take you";
then ensuring he and I became as one.

Canto XXXI

The same way as Garisenda tower appears
if looking up at its slanting side, when a
cloud goes over it in opposite direction:

so appeared Antaeus to me, as I stood
alert to his leaning, and it was such
I would have wanted to go another way.

But he placed us softly at the base
that swallows Lucifer with Judas,
nor remained long bent that way,

straightening as if he were a ship's mast.

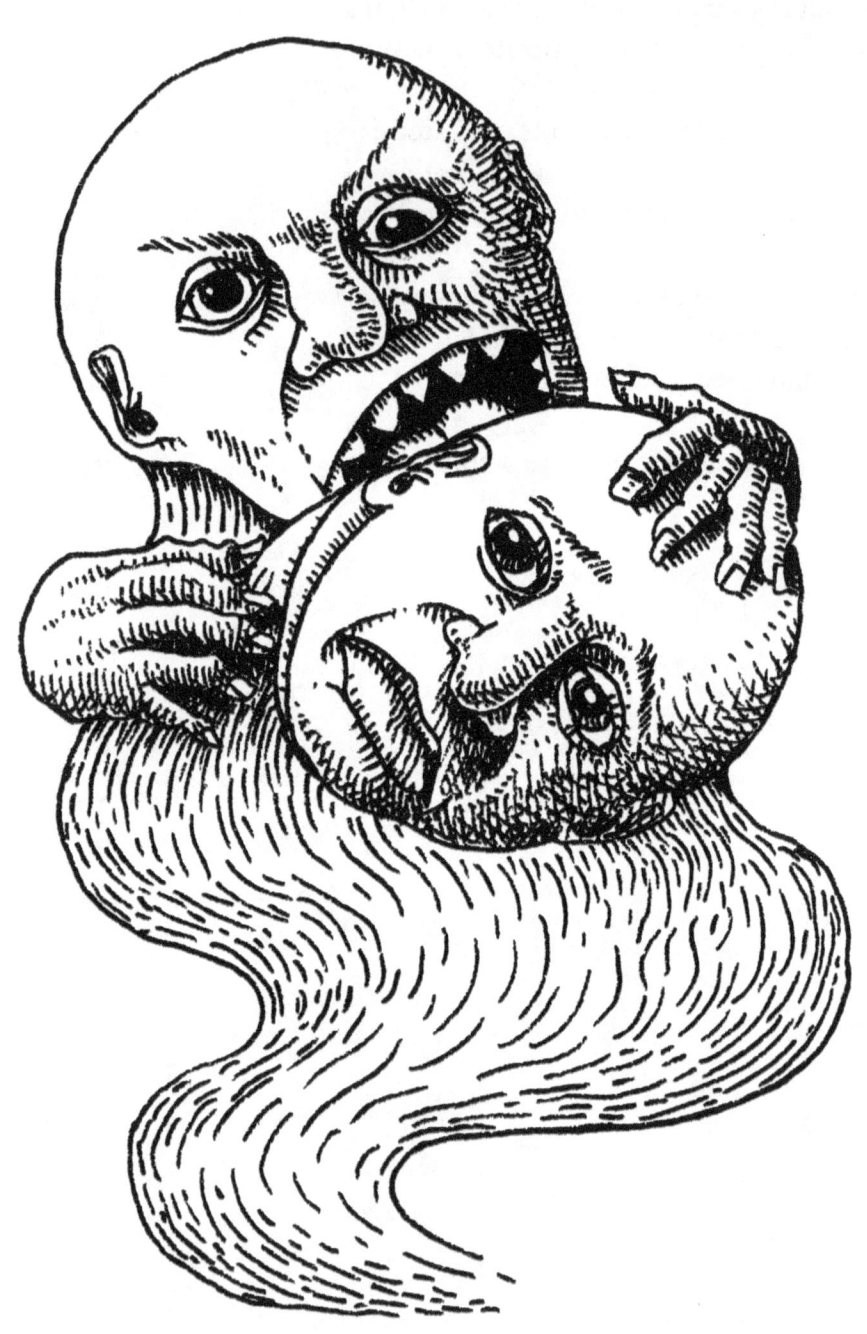

Canto XXXII

The travellers begin making their way along the ice of Cocytus (*river of lamentation* in Ancient Greek). The first of the damned they see are in the *Caïna* area of Cocytus in which traitors are embedded face down and up to their cheeks in the ice. Dante encounters the first two who are wedded chest to chest and butt heads like goats. He asks them who they are and another soul whose ears are frozen off replies that they are brothers and no others in Caïna deserve punishment more than they. The travellers continue to the next part of Cocytus called Antenora when Dante accidentally strikes a head with his foot and thus begins a contentious exchange between Dante and Bocca degli Abati. Bocca utterly refuses to give Dante his name, even under threat of having his locks torn out. Not unexpectedly, his attempt at anonymity is betrayed and he perpetuates the betrayal by naming Buoso da Duera, Tesauro dei Beccheria, Gianni de' Soldanier, Ganelon, and Tibbald. The next gruesome scene has Dante witness one soul gnawing at the head of another.

Dante's Inferno

If I had verses that were crude and jarring,
which would be suited to this awful hole
on which impinge all other rocky circles,

I would extract the essence of my vision
completely; but, as I do not have them,
not without fear do I resolve to speak:

as describing the core of all the universe
is not something to be treated lightly,
nor as a tongue uttering mummy or daddy.

May those ladies who assisted Amphion
to enclose Thebes' walls help my poetry
so my words do not divert from the facts.

Oh ill-begotten horde, more than all
others in that unspeakable place,
better had you been sheep or goats!

As soon as we were inside the dark pit
much lower than the feet of the giant,
as I still looked up at the high wall,

I heard said to me: "Mind your step:
move in a way you do not tread on the
heads of the worn wretched fraternity".

At which I turned and saw before me
and underfoot a lake that being frozen
seemed made of glass and not water.

The Danube's course in Austria during
winter did not have such a thick veil,
nor did the Don under its freezing sky,

Canto XXXII

as down there; so that if the Tambernic
or Pietrapana had fallen on it, it would
not have creaked even at the outer edge.

And as a frog croaks with mouth out
of water, when the peasant woman
is dreaming of her harvest gleaning,

so the damned souls were blue with cold
frozen in ice up to where shame blushes,
teeth chattering as does a stork's beak.

Each one of their faces was downcast;
the cold being evident in their mouths
and heart's anguish seen in their eyes.

After having looked around me a little,
I peered down at our feet and observed
two souls so tight their hair had fused.

"Tell me, you who join chests so tightly",
said I, "who are you?". Bending their necks;
and having raised their faces toward me,

their eyes previously wet with tears now
dripping to their lips, the cold freezing
the tears in the eyes and sealing them.

Steel never clamped one wood to another
so firmly, as they who like two rams so
completely overcome with rage, butted.

And another who had lost both his ears
from the cold, though with head down,
said: "Why do you look at us so intently?

Dante's Inferno

If you want to know who those two are,
they and their father Albert owned the valley
through which the river Bisenzio descends.

They came from one womb; and if searching
all of Caïna, you will not find a shadow
more deserving to be lodged in gelatine:

not he whose chest and shadow were
speared by a blow at the hand of Arthur;
nor Focaccia; nor he blocking my way

with his head, stopping me seeing ahead,
who was called Sassol Mascheroni; and if
you're Tuscan, you know him all too well.

And so you do not compel me to speak
more, know that I was Camicione dei Pazzi;
awaiting Carlin so my guilt seems less grave".

I then saw a thousand canine faces blue
from the cold; over which I cringe, and
always will, if encountering a frozen pond.

And as we walked towards the centre
upon which do gravitate all weights,
and I shivered in the eternal freeze,

if it was divine will, destiny or by chance,
I do not know; but while walking among
the heads, my foot struck hard at a face.

Crying he scolded: "Why do you kick me?
unless you come to augment retribution
for Montaperti, why molest me so?".

Canto XXXII

And I: "My Master, wait on me here,
so I may remove doubt about this one;
then hurry me up as much as you wish".

The guide remained still, and I to he
that was still wildly imprecating said:
"Who are you to reprimand others so?".

"Rather, who are you going about Antenora,
kicking", he replied, "another's face such
that were I alive, it would not be tolerated?".

"I am the one alive, and it may serve you",
was my reply, "if you wish to have fame,
that I make a mental note of your name".

And he: "I strongly crave to the contrary.
Get out of here and stop annoying me,
as your flattery's worthless on this plain!".

Then I took him by the scruff of the neck
and said: "You'd better tell me your name,
or there won't be a hair left up here,

And he to me: "Though you leave me bald,
I'll never tell you who I am, or show my face,
even if you stomp on my head a thousand times".

I already had his hair twisted in my hand,
and ripped out more than one lock,
while he bayed with eyes kept down,

when another shouted: "What's up, Bocca?
isn't a noisy jaw enough that you must
also bay? What the devil's up with you?".

"Now", I said, "not another word,
vile traitor; to add to your shame
I will pass on the truth about you".

"Get lost", he said, "and say what you like;
but do not be silent, if you exit from here,
of he who just now had such ready tongue.

He cries over French silver received:
"I saw", you can say: "he of Duera
there where sinners are cooling off".

If you are asked "Who else was there?",
by your side you have he from Beccheria,
whose throat was sawn by Florence.

Further on I think are Gianni dei
Soldanieri, Gano and Tebaldello, who
opened Faenza's doors while it slept.

We had already departed from him,
when I saw two souls frozen in a hole,
so one head was as a cap for the other;

as bread is eaten when hungry,
so the one above gnawed at the other
where the brain and spine meet:

no differently Tydeus out of hatred
did chew Menalippus' head, as did
this one the other's skull and flesh.

"Oh you who in so beastly a fashion
vent your hatred on he whom you eat,
tell me why", I said, "with this agreement,

Canto XXXII

that if you lament justly about him,
knowing who you are and of his sin,
I may reciprocate on the earth above,

unless my tongue dries out".

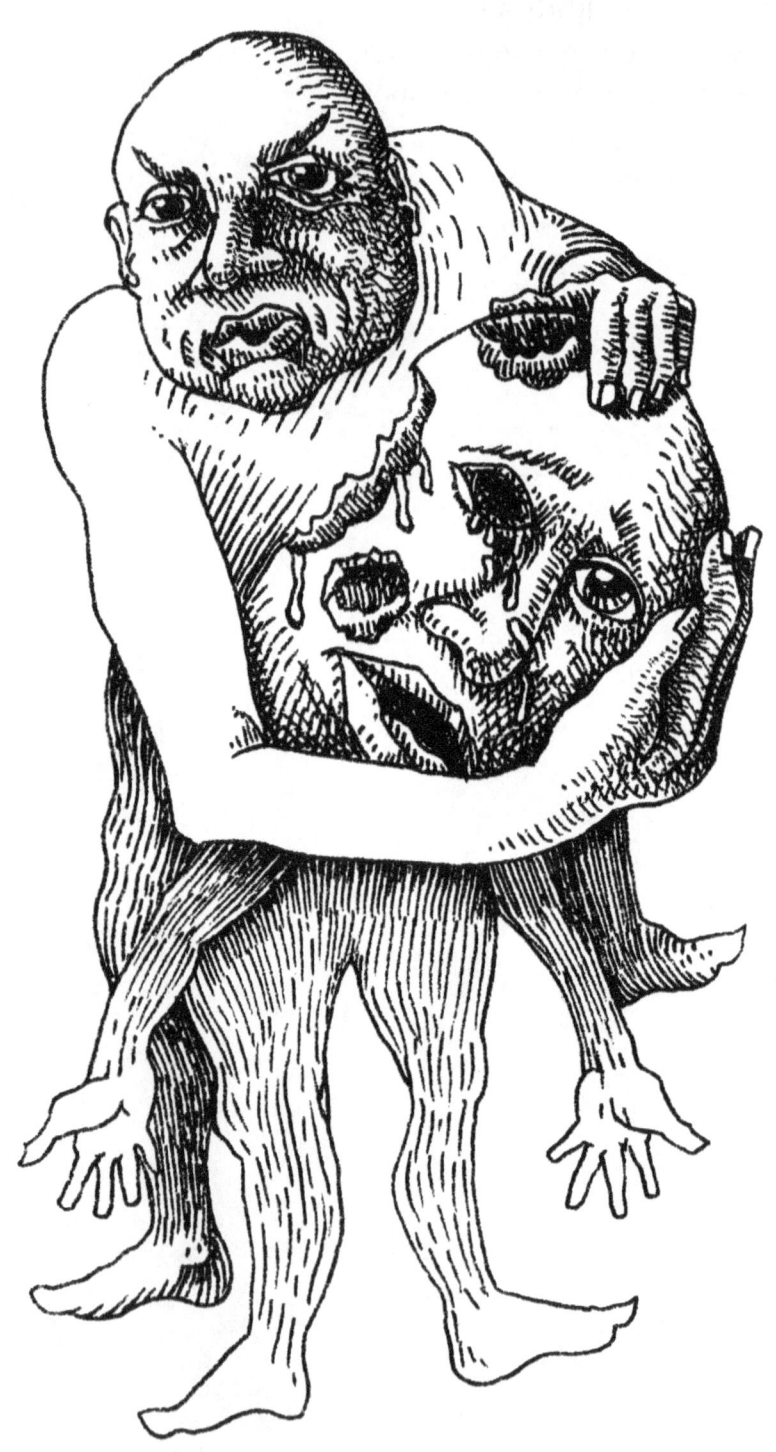

Canto XXXIII

The two souls eternally bonded are Count Ugolino and Archbishop Ruggieri, with the former feeding on the head of the latter. Count Ugolino communicates the circumstances that led to his despair. Namely, that the Archbishop had caused him to be imprisoned and starve to death along with his blameless sons. The starvation and despair take their literal consequence in the Count eternally chewing on the head of the Archbishop. Dante proceeds into the Tolomea area of Cocytus. Here are placed those who betrayed guests and Dante meets Friar Alberigo whose damned soul relates how his body still functions on earth while possessed by a demon. Dante does not believe him and refuses to fulfil the promise of removing the iced tears from his eyes if he were to tell Dante his name.

Dante's Inferno

That sinner lifted his mouth from the
bestial repast, wiping it on the hair of
the nape that he had laid waste to.

He then began: "You wish me to renew
desperate dolour that crushes my heart
just in thinking it, before speaking of it.

But if my words are to be the seed bearing
the fruit of infamy for the traitor I gnaw,
you will see me speak and cry together.

I know not who you are nor in what way
you arrived down here; but you do seem
from listening to you to be truly Florentine.

You must know that I was Count Ugolino,
and this is Archbishop Ruggieri: I will now
explain why I am close to him in this way.

There is no need to introduce you to
his malicious intriguing, that trusting
him, I was captured and put to death.

So, you will hear what you cannot have
heard, of how cruel my death was, you
will hear, and know if he did me wrong.

The tiny windowlet inside of the mew
nicknamed after me: tower of hunger,
where others are still to be locked in,

enabled me to see through its opening
many new moons, when a fateful dream
of the future tore its veil asunder.

Canto XXXIII

This one was guide and Lord, hunting
the wolf and its cubs on the mount on
whose account Pisans cannot see Lucca.

On the front line he put the Gualandi and
the Sismondi and Lanfranchi with bitches
that were ravenous, eager and trained.

After a brief run father and sons appeared
tired and I was able to see that those
sharp fangs were lacerating their sides.

When I woke up before dawn, I could
hear my children with me crying while
they were asleep, calling out for bread.

You are truly cruel if you don't feel sorrow
thinking what my heart was pre-empting;
and if you don't cry, what makes you do so?

Now they had woken and the time was
approaching that our food was brought,
and each doubted it due to their dreams;

and I heard nailing of the door beneath
the terrible tower, at which I looked
at my children's faces without a word.

I was not crying, pain having petrified me:
they were crying; and my Anselmuccio
said: "Father, why do you look at us so?".

So I did not cry nor did I respond
the entire day and following night,
until the sun rose next morning.

Dante's Inferno

As soon as a touch of sunlight appeared
in the dolorous cell, and I recognised
in the four faces my own physical state,

I bit both my hands out of anguish;
and they, thinking I was doing that
out of hunger, immediately got up

and said: "Father, it will hurt us much less
if you eat us: you did provide us this
miserable flesh, so you can deprive us".

I then settled to not make them sadder;
that day and the next we were all silent;
oh hard earth, why didn't you open up?

When we had arrived at the fourth day,
Gaddo threw himself headlong at my feet,
saying: "My Father, why not help me?".

There he died; and as you can see me,
so I saw the other three fall one by one
between the fifth and sixth days; so I,

already blind, groped over each of them,
calling them for two days after their deaths.
Then, hunger more than grief overcame me".

After having said this, with sinister eyes
he again took to the miserable skull,
with teeth strong as a dog's on a bone.

Oh Pisa, shame of the people of that
wonderful land where 'yes' echoes,
so neighbours are slow to punish you,

Canto XXXIII

may Capraia and the Gorgona move,
and obstruct the mouth of the Arno,
so that it drown your every citizen.

Even if claims were true Count Ugolino
betrayed by ceding castles, you should
not have put his sons on such a cross.

Their youth made them innocent oh new
Thebes: Uguiccione and Brigata and
the other two the canto mentions above.

We moved further, to where the ice
cruelly envelopes the other damned,
who did not face down but upwards.

The crying itself does not let them cry,
and tears being impeded at the eyes,
turn within to compound the anguish;

indeed the first tears are knotted
and just as if were crystal visors,
fill up the sockets below the brow.

And though, as in the case of a
callous, the cold took away all
sensation from my facial area,

it still seemed I could feel some wind;
so I asked: "Master, why this movement?
isn't atmospheric shift gone down here?".

And he to me: "Shortly you will be where
your eyes will give you the answer to this,
in seeing what pelts down this gust".

Dante's Inferno

And one of the anguished caked in ice
shouted out at us: "Oh such cruel spirits
that have been assigned this last posting,

take off these hard veils from my face, so
I may relieve the pain filling my heart,
a little, before the tears freeze once again".

I then said: "If you wish me to assist you,
tell me who you are: if I don't free them,
may I go to the bottom of the ice field".

He then replied: " I am friar Alberigo;
he of the fruits of the garden of evil,
here getting dates for the figs I gave".

"Oh" I said, "are you already dead?".
And he: "How my body fares in
the world above, I do not know.

This area Tolomea has this benefit,
that many times the soul falls into it
before Atropos has called it a day.

And so that you remove more willingly
the glassy tears from my face,
know that, as soon as the soul betrays

as did I, its body gets taken by
a demon, who is its custodian
until its time on earth expires.

It falls precipitously into this cistern;
and perhaps the body is still up there
of the spirit wintering here behind me.

Canto XXXIII

You should know, if you've just arrived:
he is Ser Branca d'Oria, and it has been
several years that he is thus put away".

"I believe", I said to him, "you deceive me;
because Branca d'Oria is not as yet dead,
and eats and drinks and sleeps and dresses".

"In the pit above, of the Malebranche",
he said, "where boils the viscous pitch,
Michel Zanche had not as yet arrived,

but he had left the devil in his stead
within his body, as did a kinsman of his
conducting the same betrayal with him.

Therefore now extend your hand this way;
and open my eyes". And I did not do so;
and rudeness was a courtesy in his regard.

Oh Genovesi, you men alienated from
any good custom and full of every vice,
why aren't you eradicated from the world?".

Indeed I found one of you alongside
the worst of Romagna, whose soul
by its works now bathes in Cocytus,

and in body seems still alive on earth.

Canto XXXIV

The final Canto of *Inferno* reaches the apex of horror and consequence of human treachery. Dante had noticed a wind in the previous Canto notwithstanding his expectation that the atmospheric environment was a static one. As indicated by Virgil, he comes to understand here that it is generated by the movement of Lucifer's wings. Lucifer himself is embedded in ice up to the chest, suggesting immobility and utter impotence. Souls are buried in ice in completely random positions. Lucifer has three faces and in each mouth he masticates on the worst traitors of humanity: Judas, Brutus and Cassius.

"The ensigns of the king of hell advance
toward us; therefore look ahead of you",
said my Master, "if you can discern him".

Just as when a heavy fog is forming,
or when night falls in our hemisphere,
afar appears a mill driven by the wind,

there then appeared to me such a device;
and from the wind I sought refuge behind
my guide, since there was no other retreat.

There I was, and fearfully I put it in verse,
where all of the souls were submerged,
and appeared as pieces of straw in glass.

Some are lying down; others are erect,
one with his head, another with his soles;
others arched with faces at their feet.

When we had progressed far enough,
that it pleased my Master to show me
the creature of once beauteous a form,

he moved from in front and stopped me,
"Here is Dis", he said, "and here the place
where you must be armed with courage".

Do not ask, reader, how I became frozen
and speechless, as I will not write of it,
as every word would be inadequate.

I found I was neither dead nor alive;
so think, if you have an ounce of wit,
how I became, denied one and the other.

Canto XXXIV

The emperor of the kingdom of pain
protruded from the ice above his breast;
and I am nearer to the size of a giant,

than giants are to the size of his arms:
think then proportional to that body part
what the complete dimensions must be.

If he was as beautiful then as ugly now,
having at his creator cocked his brow,
it is right all grief should come from him.

Oh how stupefying it was to me
when I saw three faces on his head!
One was in front and was vermillion;

the other two that joined this one
were half way along each shoulder,
and met at the crest of his head:

the right one seemed of white and yellow;
the one on the left such, it was as they
from where the Nile descends to a valley.

From under each came two large wings,
being appropriate for such a colossal bird:
I have never seen ships' sails of that size.

They had no feathers, but were like
those of a bat; and they flapped,
so three winds emanated from them:

therefore all of Cocytus was kept frozen.
He cried with six eyes, down three chins
dripping tears mixed with bloody drool.

Dante's Inferno

In each mouth his teeth ground a sinner,
with the actions of a scutch, in this way
tormenting all three of them at once.

To the one in front the biting was naught
compared to the clawing, that sometimes
left the skin on his back completely flayed.

"That soul up there suffering greatest pain",
said my Master, "is Judas Iscariot, with
head inside and dangling legs outside.

As for the other two with heads protruding,
he that hangs from the black snout is Brutus:
see how he contorts and says not a word!;

the other is Cassius, seeming so muscular.
But it is nearly night time and we now
must head off, having seen all there is".

As he wanted me to, I embraced his neck;
and he waited on the best time and place,
and when the wings were opened enough,

he latched onto the hairy flanks;
tuft after tuft he descended then
between thick fur and frozen crust.

When we arrived where the thigh
pivots, at the outer part of the hips,
the guide, with effort and breathless,

turned his head to where the legs were,
and gripped the fur as a man climbing,
so that I thought we were returning to hell.

Canto XXXIV

"Hold on tightly that by such stairs",
said Master, panting like a man wearied:
"we must depart from so much evil".

He then got out from a cleft in the rock
and placed me on the edge to be seated;
carefully making his way towards me.

I lifted my gaze and thought to see
Lucifer in the same way I left him,
yet I saw his legs being held upwards;

and if I then did suffer from anguish,
the vulgar should reflect, as do not see
the nature of the point I did traverse.

"Up you get", Master said, "on your feet:
the road is long and the walk hard going,
and the sun is returning to middle tierce".

This was not a palace hallway where
we were, rather a subterranean vault
with a rugged floor and of dim light.

"Before extricating myself from the abyss
my Master", I said when I straightened,
"talk to me some to free me from error:

where is the ice field? And how can he be
fixed upside down? And how in so few hours,
did the sun travel from night to morning?".

And he said: "you imagine still being on
the other side of centre, where I gripped
the hair of the evil worm who pierces earth.

Dante's Inferno

You were there throughout my descent;
when I turned, you moved past that point
to which weights everywhere are drawn.

And you're now under the hemisphere
opposite to that covering the great dry
expanse and beneath whose zenith was

the man born who lived without sin;
your feet are on a small circular area
that is on the opposite side of Judecca.

When here it is morning, there is evening;
and he, whose hair became our ladder,
is still embedded as he was there before.

He fell down from Heaven on this side;
and the land that earlier extended here,
for fear of him veiled itself undersea,

and came to our hemisphere; and maybe
fleeing him, the land appearing here left
this empty void when it shot upwards".

Down there is a place far from Beelzebub
as distant as hell extends, that is not
found by sight, but by the sound

of a streamlet that descends there
through a path it has carved in rock,
in a spiralling slightly sloping course.

My guide and I took that hidden walk-
way to return to the world of light;
and without seeking any repose at all,

Canto XXXIV

we scaled up, he ahead and I behind,
till I saw through a crevice some
beautiful things held in the sky.

So we came out to again see the stars.

Wakefield Press is an independent publishing and
distribution company based in Adelaide, South Australia.
We love good stories and publish beautiful books.
To see our full range of books, please visit our website at
www.wakefieldpress.com.au
where all titles are available for purchase.
To keep up with our latest releases, news and events,
subscribe to our monthly newsletter.

Find us!

Facebook: www.facebook.com/wakefield.press
Twitter: www.twitter.com/wakefieldpress
Instagram: www.instagram.com/wakefieldpress

www.ingramcontent.com/pod-product-compliance
Lightning Source LLC
Chambersburg PA
CBHW030822230426
43667CB00008B/1328